MW01293885

Moments of Impact

Moments of Impact

By Tom Wilson

Contributing Editor Stephen Quesnelle

Copyright 2015 by Tom Wilson and Stephen Quesnelle

Library of Congress Cataloguing-in-Publication Data

All rights reserved under International and Pan-American Copyright Conventions. No part of this publication may be stored in a database or retrieval system or reproduced, distributed, or transmitted in any form by any means, including photocopying, scanning, recording, or other mechanical or electronic methods, without the prior written permission of the publishers, except in the case of brief quotations embodied in critical reviews and certain other non-commercial uses permitted by copyright law. For permission requests, contact The International Safety Institute at www.insafein.com

Copy Editing by Claire Morris
Cover Design by Cheryl Perez
Front cover photo by Lasha Paramchuk
Back photo cover photo by Stephen Quesnelle
Book Design by Cheryl Perez: yourepublished.com

The International Safety Institute
www.insafein.com

ISBN 978-1-51176826-9

First Edition
April 2015

DEDICATION

This book is dedicated to the seven men who lost their lives on November 16, 2008, and to their many family members and friends who loved them dearly.

In memory of:

Kyle Adams

Jerry Burns

Ajay Cariappa

Wally Klemens

Peter McLeod

Tom Orgar

Matt Sawchenko

A portion of all book proceeds will be donated to the University of Alberta Hospital Burn Ward.

ACKNOWLEDGEMENTS

Thanks to all those who took the time to review early copies of the manuscript or provided other helpful advice along the way:

Dr. Judy Agnew	Heather MacLeod
Lise Bolen	Alanna Moores
Lisa Cantwell	Laletha (Lita) Nithiyanandan
Cam Carson	Megan Omar
Bob Chelmick	Terry O'Keefe
Dale Danylchuk	Lasha Paramchuk
Mike Daley	Noreen Quesnelle
Francisco Gomez	Linda Sawchenko
Steve Hicks	Geoff Smith
Susan Hicks	Lee Ann Smith
Brett Holbrook	Jody Sveistrup
Bob Kula	Isobel Wilson

Thanks to the local hunters Al "Bunny" Hailey and Fred Severre for alerting local authorities to the sound of a plane crash on Thormanby Island.

Thanks to the members of the Royal Canadian Marine Search and Rescue Team, in particular Ron Dinsdale, Peter Forster, George Lyske, Bob McKee, Drew McKee and Alan Skelley.

Thanks to the Sunshine Coast Search and Rescue team, in particular Alec Tebbutt and Richard Till.

Thanks to the doctors and nurses at Vancouver General Hospital and to all the doctors and nurses at the burn ward at the University of Alberta Hospital.

Special thanks to Kris Burns, Dan Bourque and Jodi Murphy for building the memorial cross that I took to the Thormanby Island crash site.

IN MEMORY OF THOSE LOST

Kyle Adams

Kyle, 29, graduated from the University of New Brunswick in 2002 and became the owner of Noah's Pet Store, an endeavour that was as much a labour of love as it was a business venture. In 2005 Kyle moved to Edmonton to work for Peter Kiewit and Sons Company. Kyle's family described him as a man with a *"gentle smile that could melt the hearts of those around him and he will be forever loved and remembered for his inner strength and his quiet, kind ways. Anyone who knew Kyle considers themselves fortunate to have had the opportunity to know him and to love him."*

Jerry Burns

Jerry, 42, was born on December 25, and to his sisters he was the "Christmas baby". A lifelong Squamish, BC resident, Jerry left behind his wife Carrie and two children: 13-year-old stepdaughter Jessica and five-year-old daughter Taylor. Friend Ivan Jensen remembers him as *"a joker who loved to do funny things. It was always a good time when we got to spend some time together. We enjoyed riding our ATVs, mountain biking, fishing, walking our dogs and camping."*

Ajay Cariappa

Ajay's mother Lekha Chengappa wrote:

*"In one of the stars I shall be living, in one of them I shall be laughing
And in the laughter of all the stars, you will see me always.*

*"These are the thoughts that we shall carry with us while remembering
our dear son Ajay who will remain in our hearts forever.*

*"Ajay was born on July 17, 1974 in Mysore, a city in South India. He
started his schooling from Bangalore and later at various cities as his parents
moved to their native village to look after their coffee plantations. As we
reminisce his journey of life, we recollect with pride Ajay as a meticulous and
obedient child whose years at the Ramakrishna Vidyashala at Mysore
groomed him to be a person with great strength of character, integrity,
courage and compassion.*

*"He completed his Bachelor's in Civil Engineering from the prestigious
National Institute of Engineering, Mysore. He left India in 1997 to pursue his
Master's from the University of New Brunswick in Construction and Planning.
Ajay's colleagues remember his first day at work, where they said, 'We noticed
a quiet, well-mannered young man totally in awe at the beauty of the Columbia
valley. His eyes grew wide and he grinned from ear to ear as he surveyed the
place.'*

*"Ajay's first priority in life was his work, which he'd describe in great
detail to his parents. He had a personality of his own and poured his heart into
everything he set his mind to.*

*"Ajay's love for food and fine dining made him the hearty man that he
was and his Indian heritage stuck out both in his art of cooking and serving
his many friends in Canada who fondly remember him for that. His love for
the outdoors was evident in his fishing expeditions and his game of golf. He
spent a lot of his free time reading and had a large collection of books. He
loved travelling and visited his cousins in the US and UK.*

"He became a citizen of Canada because he loved the place. He had many cousins in the US who tried to persuade him to move there, but he would always tell us that he loved Canada.

"To us, his parents and his family and friends who loved him, he will always be remembered as the burly, happy, helpful and smiling child. His memory lingers, and we believe Ajay has just moved on into another dimension, into another world.

"A heart of gold stopped beating, hardworking hands at rest,
God broke our hearts to prove to us he only takes the best.
The leaves and flowers may wither; the golden sun may set,
But the hearts that loved so dearly are the ones who won't forget."

Waldemar (Walter) Klemens

Walter was 24, and lived in Red Deer, Alberta. Friend Robert Mason said, *"He was one of those infectious people with more passion for life than anyone I've ever met. I've never known him to have a bad day in his life. He was always full of life."*

Peter McLeod

Peter McLeod, 54, was a veteran coastal pilot who had recently joined Pacific Coastal Airlines. He was well known by most seasoned water pilots in the Oz seaplane scene after decades flying the Australian coastal waterways in many states.

After leaving Australia on a two-year adventure around the world, flying the J-34 Mallard aircraft that he loved so much, Peter settled down in Vancouver, Canada with his partner Lynn, and began flying west coast charters.

Tom Orgar

Tom was 29 at the time of the crash, and an employee of Finning Tractor in Surrey, British Columbia.

His wife Megan wrote: *"Taken far too soon, we all carry on living life the way Tom did. Putting 100 percent into everything we do and enjoying every moment like it could be our last. Every day we wake up missing him like he left yesterday, but we also wake up grateful for the lives we have that he contributed so greatly to. He was and always will be a wonderful husband, son, brother, uncle and friend. One that is loved, respected and missed deeply every second of every day."*

Matt Sawchenko

Matt, 26, left behind his pregnant fiancée, and was on his way to his first day of work at Toba Inlet that day.

Matt's mother Linda wrote: "Where does one begin when trying to write about a young man so special, no words can describe. Matty was born in Penticton, BC on May 19, 1982, and grew up with his brothers Kirk and Ryan riding dirt bikes, water-skiing and spending hours finding the best snow at Big White Ski Resort near Kelowna. He loved his family and loved to be outdoors with them exploring and enjoying the mountains, rivers and lakes of British Columbia.

"One of Matty's many gifts was his ability to bring sunshine and smiles into any encounter – he just had a way of spreading happiness and seeing the positive in every situation! It seems some are too special to stay long in this world, and Matty was one who had no chance to grow old. In his special, ever-caring way, Matty left us an amazing gift to hold onto and continue his song. Matty's beautiful baby boy, Matthew Junior, blessed our world when he was born April 2, 2009.

In the dark hours of Nov 16, 2008

"Oh please come more quickly early morning light, we must work so swiftly to discover the flight. There is someone so special out there in the night, And he needs to come home to help make things right.

There are few with the gifts our beautiful Matthew had, And today it is true the whole world is sad. The air it feels cooler and the silence too deep, It just isn't possible for any of us to sleep.

The stars will shine brighter in the cold nights ahead, And we will hug one another as we head off to bed. A young man so special no words can describe, Our Matthew lives on in these words as I scribe.

He loved oh so deeply in his very special way, And so many are richer whom he touched every day. Matt will live on with us and help us along, As we struggle to get by missing him and his song.

Some are too special to stay long in this world, And our Matthew is one who had no chance to grow old. In his wonderful, special way as he moves on, He leaves us a new life growing to continue his song."

TABLE OF CONTENTS

PROLOGUE

The pilot held open the door of the Grumman Goose seaplane at Vancouver International Airport as I climbed aboard with six of my co-workers on the damp and foggy morning of Sunday, November 16, 2008. I recognized our pilot, Peter, from having made this trip a few times to the remote construction site at Toba Inlet, where we were headed to relieve another crew.

The small floatplane was old, cramped, noisy and uncomfortable. I just wanted sleep, so that is what I did: I put in earplugs, curled my six-foot frame up into the fetal position in the window seat of row 2 and went to sleep for 20 minutes. I bolted awake to the loud sound of something bashing into our aircraft. Flying low through the fog in the mountainous area, our pilot had strayed from course. As treetops began ripping into the underbelly of the plane, he applied full power to the engines and pulled back on the stick, commanding the powerful craft to climb higher. It was too late. The wings were already mortally wounded. A split second later, we slammed into the rugged side of a mountainous island at full throttle.

Impact.

A brief moment of impact.

The moment of impact knocked me temporarily unconscious.

When I regained consciousness, the plane was a burning shell, shattered and smashed beyond recognition.

The impact was so violent that the aircraft's emergency locator beacon – a device specifically designed to survive crashes and alert search and rescue teams – was destroyed. No one knew we were here.

The crash had ruptured the nearly full fuel tanks, showering a 100-metre radius in aviation fuel. Everything around me was burning.

Still belted into my seat, I was unable to run.

My clothes and exposed skin were covered in aviation fuel.

I was on fire.

My name is Tom Wilson, and this is my story.

In the chapters ahead, I am going to share with you my thoughts on "moments of impact" throughout our lives. Some of these special moments we can create in positive and productive ways. We can positively influence the lives of those around us with brief moments of impact – connecting with others in a genuine and influential way.

Other moments are like the beginning of my journey to enlightenment. They are beyond our control and begin with horrific and tragic moments of impact: some physical, some emotional and some spiritual, all with the same potentially crushing effects. While we may not choose to have these things happen to us we DO have the power to choose how these events will, or will not, define us.

This book is written in two distinct parts. Book 1 is the story of the fateful airplane journey, what happened to those of us on that plane, and my personal journey of self-discovery and learning.

Book 2 is about the role of human behaviour in safety, and what we can all do to make the world a safer place.

BOOK 1

THE PREMONITION

Do you believe in premonitions? I can tell you that in early 2008 I did not, but looking back on that day now, I had what I can only describe as a premonition. I am not sure if having a premonition today would change my course of action, but I would give it much more consideration because of the experience that I am about to share with you. If I had changed my course of action on that November day, it might have influenced others. Maybe, just maybe, one or more of the seven good men who were with me that day might have followed my lead and still be alive today.

At noon on Saturday, November 15, 2008, I was driving to Edmonton International Airport from my home in the small community of Fort Saskatchewan, Alberta. The journey was for another work-related trip as I had done at least 100 times before; this time to the Plutonic Hydroelectric Project located at Toba Inlet in the mountains north of Vancouver. My plan was to take a commercial flight from Edmonton to Vancouver on Saturday, spend the night in a hotel, then catch a chartered floatplane to the work site early Sunday morning.

From out of nowhere, a very strong feeling came over me as if something very bad was going to happen. I felt as though I should cancel my flights and not go on this particular trip. There was no logic or reason behind this overwhelming feeling, which made it almost impossible to act upon. Nonetheless, it was there, very strong and not easily dismissed. Along the drive to the airport the premonition continued to bother me yet there was no indication of anything wrong or out of the ordinary. I had taken many similar trips before, so there was nothing to be afraid of. Even though I had no real reason to cancel my travel plans, this feeling of uneasiness had me considering it. I tried to defeat the bad feeling by using logic, and I talked myself out of any thoughts of cancelling this trip. *What could I possibly tell my boss?* I thought. *That I had a "bad feeling" and decided I wasn't going on this trip?* The nagging feeling just didn't make any logical sense to me, but I continued to wrestle with these thoughts as I went on my way to the airport.

At the time, I was a business manager going into my eighth year with Peter Kiewit Sons', a very large global construction company. I had managed to climb the corporate ladder from an entry-level position to that of an area manager responsible for reporting on the financial performance of various construction projects. In this role it was common to travel directly to construction sites, some of which were in very remote locations.

I had made this specific trip easily a couple of times before; my past experience and familiarity with the route caused me to question the premonition. The first flight to Vancouver went smoothly, and after landing safely in Vancouver, I dismissed the uneasy feeling completely.

The lack of incident helped me justify that the uneasy feeling held no real meaning. Little did I know what was about to take place the very next morning.

Once in Vancouver, I went to the hotel to meet up with my friend and co-worker Kyle Adams. Kyle was a bright 29-year-old man at the time. I had been working closely with him for the past year, and we had developed a friendship. This was Kyle's first work trip to any remote project, and his first flight ever on a floatplane. Over dinner that evening, he talked excitedly about the trip. Kyle had an interest in floatplanes, and had done some research on the history of the Grumman Goose amphibious aircraft we would be taking in the morning. I was surprised at how much he had learned about this particular plane and how much he was looking forward to taking this trip. Looking back on our dinner, and the last night of Kyle's life, it was ironic that he was so excited to take this particular flight.

8 a.m.: The next morning, Sunday, November 16, 2008, we met in the lobby to check out of the hotel and get a cab to the airport. Outside the weather was very foggy and accompanied by a light drizzle of rain. On the way, we discussed the possibility of the flight being cancelled, but decided to continue to the airport to find out the status of our flight firsthand. If it did take off, we would be on it. There were a limited number of flights in and out of Toba Inlet, so if our flight was cancelled we would likely just have to wait around the airport until the conditions cleared up anyway.

9 a.m.: The small South Terminal of the Vancouver airport is used for smaller private planes and charter aircraft. Off to the south side of the runway is a ramp down to an inlet on the Pacific Ocean that provides access to water for amphibious planes. When we got to the counter of the charter airline, some other passengers were already there. They told us that the flight was delayed due to the weather but would be taking off shortly so not to go far.

I recognized another co-worker, Ajay Cariappa, as one of those in line. Since we had some time on our hands before the flight departed, Kyle and I invited Ajay to join us for breakfast. I remember that breakfast very clearly. It all seemed so normal. It is hard to believe that Kyle and Ajay would die that morning. Remembering the normality of that breakfast with my friends drives home the reality of never knowing when death is coming. I still feel that it was unfair that there was no warning of tragic events looming ahead.

9:45 a.m.: From the airport restaurant we saw the others lining up at the door leading out to the runway. We quickly paid our bill, grabbed our luggage and headed for the door. Moments later, we were given the signal to head out across the runway to the airplane.

Making the way toward the little eight-passenger floatplane, I took note of the poor weather conditions. I was quite surprised, as I think we all were, that we were being directed to board the plane even though the conditions hadn't improved. I wondered why the flight had been initially delayed if we were going to take off in these conditions anyway. There seemed to be a sense of uneasiness amongst us, but we all kept our thoughts to ourselves and continued the short walk to the plane. Once at the plane, we handed our luggage to the pilot and lined up for boarding, one by one.

This particular plane is small, with a proportionately small door for entering, unlike typical commercial aircraft. Ajay and I started toward the door at the same time, bumping into each other. We both stepped back immediately to allow the other to go first. We then continued to politely banter back and forth about who should enter first. I am very stubborn, so eventually Ajay gave in and climbed aboard. Once inside, Ajay went straight for the co-pilot seat. On these flights, passengers are allowed to sit in the co-pilot's seat – a popular choice that offers substantially more leg room and, when the weather is clear, an amazing view of the mountains. I was a little disappointed to miss out on the extra leg room up front, but that's what I got for being stubborn and insisting that Ajay board before me.

On this particular day, unbeknownst to either of us, it was also a sad factor in the difference between life and death.

I boarded right behind Ajay, and chose the seat two rows behind the pilot, underneath the left wing. Unlike larger commercial aircraft, the wings on floatplanes are mounted above the passenger cabin. Kyle boarded next, and took the seat directly behind me. Looking out and into the fog, less than half of the runway was visible. It didn't feel very reassuring, but I kept comforting myself by thinking that the pilot was obviously okay with it. Looking back at how normal this moment seemed is also a little disturbing. The other guys were chatting a little, looking out their windows and fidgeting in their seats just as they would on any other flight. This is another snapshot in my memory that reminds me of how quickly and unexpectedly our life journey can take a cruel turn.

Peter, our pilot, was the last to board. He made his way to the front of the plane and took his seat in the cockpit. Immediately after putting on his headset, he looked back into the passenger cabin and said:

"Guys, we are going to have to do some low-level flying because of the weather conditions. If anyone has a problem with that, let me know now and I will let you off."

The awkward silence following that statement echoed throughout the plane. We all just looked at one another without a word said.

Then, breaking the silence, Peter added:

"It is my job to keep this flight boring. If anything gets exciting at all we will just turn around, come back, and have coffee."

Although we were all still feeling uneasy, Peter's second statement comforted us enough to break the tension of the moment. We all looked at one other again, nodded in agreement, and gave the thumbs up. Out of all the things I am going to tell you, it is this moment, this second in time, this opportunity that I had to speak up and chose not to, that will haunt me for the rest of my life.

It was a moment of impact squandered away.

It is also the moment that I have learned the most from.

This was the moment that could have prevented the tragedy, but it was now past and smoothed over by the pilot's comment about returning for coffee. The moment, and the opportunity to speak up, was gone and could never be regained. Our journey and this tragedy were now underway and inevitable.

The City of Vancouver is ringed by the picturesque North Shore Mountains, which form part of the Pacific Mountain Ranges. The Pacific shoreline along the westerly coast of British Columbia is likewise dotted by the Southern Gulf Islands – a series of small, low-mountain islands. These mountains and islands along the Canadian west coast were formed approximately 130 million years ago by a combination of volcanic action and shifting of tectonic plates.

The Grumman Goose aircraft that we were on that morning. The window nearest the tail of the plane forms part of the door used to access the aircraft. The plane has small wheels underneath the fuselage to allow the craft to roll on pavement, but it is designed to take off and land on water. This picture was taken on a previous flight at the dock at Toba Inlet, which was to be our final destination. One of the many Southern Gulf Islands is visible in the background.

Photo by www.prpeak.com

ROARING THROUGH THE RAIN AND STRAIGHT INTO HELL

10 a.m.: Peter pushed a button, and the two large propellers started to turn. Both of the large 450-horsepower engines quickly barked to life. He looked back at us and motioned to ensure we had our seatbelts on and our earplugs in. These World War II-era planes were not built with passenger comfort in mind. When the engines were at full power, their roar was so loud in the passenger cabin that earplugs were mandatory. With everyone buckled up and in compliance, the engines began to rev up and the plane started to roll forward.

The Grumman Goose floatplane is designed to take off from water; on land they wobble around awkwardly like the birds that they are named after. There is a small cove in the Pacific Ocean alongside Vancouver International Airport and a security gate just off the edge of the runway that allows planes to access the launch. We cleared the gate and, like a goose, started to waddle down the gentle descent of the launch ramp toward the sea.

An airport security camera captured an image of our plane launching into the ocean.

Photo by Vancouver International Airport Security

I looked out the windows on the right side of the plane, searching for a small island about two kilometres to the northwest of the airport. On previous flights I had been nervous about the plane gaining enough altitude to clear the island; it had felt like we hadn't been much higher than the trees as we had passed by. The fog was so thick on this morning that the trees and island were entirely hidden from view.

10:13 a.m.: The plane, now fully floating in the water, turned north and started preparing for takeoff. The engines roared to full power, reverberating loudly throughout the passenger cabin. As our speed increased, the plane began to achieve some lift, making hard bounces off the choppy waves as it struggled for separation from the sea. Every second made me more anxious; I just wanted to be high up in the air and out of danger. As I focussed on the strain of the engines, the noise of water rushing under my feet subsided. We stopped bouncing off the top of the waves; I stared to relax as we continued to climb.

I peered out my window on the left side and let out a sigh of relief as the island I had been watching for appeared underneath us, as it always did. We had officially made another successful takeoff. It was now time to shift my focus to the uncomfortable flight ahead.

I pulled the hood of my sweater up over my head and started to shift around in my seat, trying to find the best angle for leg comfort. At six feet tall, there wasn't enough room in the aisle for me to stretch my legs out, so I brought my knees close to my chest, angled them to the left, and sandwiched them in between my body and the seat in front of me.

With my hood up, the window was not cold to the touch, so I rested my head against it and closed my eyes for a nap. I remember it felt like being seated in the perfect fetal position, with my head rested forward and my knees brought to my chest.

The next 15 minutes of the flight were uneventful. I would occasionally shift around, open my eyes and look down at the ocean waves rushing by only a couple of hundred feet beneath us. We were flying low, but this is what the pilot had prepared us for, so I just closed my eyes and continued trying to relax.

Without any warning – smashing the monotony of the flight – was a very loud sound. It sounded like grinding metal. My face was still pressed against the window, and as soon as I opened my eyes I could see trees. Trees right outside my window! They were close, too close –

I could have reached out and touched them. The loud grinding noise was the sound of trees slashing away at the underbelly of our plane. Stripping away the landing gear. Disembowelling the plane and spilling our luggage into the air.

Before my mind had the time to fully process what was going on, I was thrown forward, very hard, into the seat in front of me, and knocked unconscious.

10:32 a.m.: Impact.

Still in the fetal position, I remember being forced forward into the cushioned back of the seat in front of me before passing out.

This is the last thing I remember of our flight.

From seeing trees to going unconscious was but a brief moment. It was over as fast as it started. Not one person on board that flight screamed. Not one person yelled "hang on" or "holy shit". Not a sound. One second we were flying, the next instant there was darkness, fire and death.

Our plane had been flying at a low level because of the fog, low clouds and limited visibility. The only understanding of what happened at this point is the pilot lost his bearings in the fog, misjudged the flight path, and flew directly into the side of an uninhabited island. If we had been only 200 feet to the left, or 50 feet higher, everything would have been fine.

As the treetops started ripping into the body of the aircraft, the pilot lost his ability to control it. The investigation report showed that he did have time to apply full power to the engines and pull back on the stick in an effort to gain altitude quickly, but wing damage, gravity and momentum took over. Our plane crashed into the side of a mountain at approximately 150 miles per hour in a very violent manner.

The moment of impact on eight lives.

This journey, and the lives of the other seven, ended here. From out of nowhere and in the blink of an eye, their lives were over. There wasn't any indication of any kind to anyone that their lives would soon be over. No opportunity to say goodbye to loved ones, no time to say any of the things they would have wanted to. Just immediate darkness. Life can be taken in an instant, and witnessing this firsthand is the most disturbing thing that you could ever imagine. This moment of impact changed my life, as it did for the many people who loved my fellow travellers dearly. This moment was unfair, tragic and ruthless. This was the hardest moment of my life, and the beginning of a whole new journey for me.

MAN ON FIRE

After being knocked unconscious, there is often a slow grogginess to regaining consciousness. I did not regain consciousness this way. I was forced out of unconsciousness into a world of immediate pain and panic like nothing I could have ever imagined.

With my seatbelt on, and my hoodie still pulled up over my head, I shot awake screaming in pain.

I was covered in aviation fuel from head to toe, and the fuel was burning.

I was a man on fire.

Before I describe what happened next, I want you to try to understand the mental and emotional state of mind that comes with being on fire. The pain of burning alive is obvious, but it is the state of mind that is hard to understand without experiencing it.

Panic is defined as "a sudden overwhelming fear that produces hysterical and irrational behaviour". Panic inhibits one's ability to follow directions or think logically. I can tell you that when I awoke, I was in such a state of panic that I can only describe it as a complete lack of sanity. I was on fire. I was screaming at the top of my lungs in pain. My hands were burning. My legs and body were burning. I could see flames dancing all around me and in front of my face.

The intensity of the pain was indescribable. It felt like the most amount of pain that a human could possibly endure; second by second it got worse, and continued in an upward spiral of intensity.

The pain fed the panic, the panic fed emotional reaction and made me more irrational. The message your brain gets is simply that you are on fire, the pain will soon kill you, and you need to get out of the flames NOW! The sheer urgency of this message is so overwhelming that it contributes to the panic, which in turn inhibits your ability to act.

Screaming and flailing, I tried tearing at the seatbelt with my burning hands. I was fighting like an animal, just grabbing and pulling at it. Anything to get out of the fire right now. My mind was racing, yet my hands would not function logically. In that intense state of panic, my brain could remember how to unclip the seatbelt, but my body just would not follow the directions to do so.

My brain recognized that I had to do something fast, so I forced myself to sit straight up in the seat, stretch my arms and lift my hands toward the sky to get them out of the fire for an instant of relief. I tried to mentally calm myself for just a fraction of a second to regain control of my physical actions. I needed to get enough mental control to undo the seatbelt or it was over – I was about to burn to death strapped into my seat.

That "self-talk", the fraction of a second that I took to raise my arms to the sky and focus on commanding the physical actions of my hands, was a moment of impact. That fraction of a second was enough. I forced my hands back down into the flames, still wildly screaming and flailing, but this time with a concentrated focus on undoing the clip. I grabbed at the metal buckle and it released!

I shot straight up out of my seat and directly into a panicked run – screaming, burning, and losing my mind. Undoing a seatbelt was about the most complicated task I could have performed in that state of panic; if there had been more of the cabin left to maneuver through I might have been trapped inside. The cabin of the aircraft around me had been completely destroyed so, with nothing to impede me, I was able to run directly into the forest. There was no thought as to a path or particular direction to run. My immediate instinct was simply to move as fast as possible to get away from the flames. I leaned forward and started running straight ahead.

My hoodie was still pulled over my head, and it too was soaked in burning aviation fuel. As I started to run from the wreckage and pick up speed, the flames from the rim of my hood turned inward. The panic was telling my brain to make my feet run, but in doing so the motion created a wind that was pushing flames directly into my face. While still running, I grabbed at my flaming hoodie and I wrestled it over my head and off my body. Screaming, still burning, I next realized that my jeans were also on fire. I started to jump around madly, slapping at the flames with my raw pulpy hands until the flames were out.

With all the flames on my body now extinguished, I stopped jumping and just stood there, naked from the waist up, arms raised to the sky, screaming. I screamed, and I screamed; I screamed longer and harder than I ever thought possible. I was in so much pain.

I was now out of immediate danger, but badly burned, and poorly clothed for a cold November day. People often ask me what I was thinking through all of this. The answer is quite simple; in that kind of situation you don't think, you only react. My brain had been so overloaded with panic that it hadn't even registered yet that we had been in a plane crash. I didn't know anything other than I was on fire and in intense, excruciating pain. In that situation my brain didn't have the capacity to question where I was or why I was on fire. The panic and pain were robbing me of any rational thought.

Numb from shock, I staggered about 30 metres from the crash site and stood facing into the forest when I heard a loud explosion behind me. I felt both heat and pressure waves press against my back. Oddly, the explosion really didn't get much of my attention at all; I was barely aware of it, and still fighting to gain control of my thoughts and actions.

As time passed, the panic started to slowly subside, allowing some rational thought to return. It was like fighting to get out of the foggy semi-consciousness of a nightmare; it seemed like an eternity.

I held my hands in front of my face, staring at them in horror. The skin of my fingers and most of the back of my hands was completely burnt off. There were large chunks of burnt flesh hanging from the back of my hands and my fingers. There were strands of skin hanging down in front of my eyes. The tip of my nose was the same raw meaty red as my hands. My face was generating as much pain as my hands, so even without a mirror I knew that it was severely burnt as well. Looking down, I noticed an eight-inch gash across my stomach. The gash was not generating enough pain compared to everything else to be a concern.

As my senses began working again, I started to notice the overpowering stench of something rotten. It is hard to describe the smell of burnt flesh, but knowing that the smell was coming from my own body made me feel sick.

Without the overloading messages of panic, my brain was slowly being freed up to process my surroundings. I started to feel the cold breeze; it was the middle of November, and I was on a coastal island off Vancouver, BC, Canada. It was only 8°C (46°F), drizzling rain, foggy and windy. I was seriously burnt and wearing only jeans and work boots. I started to shiver, still in shock, and trying to sort things out in my head.

What the hell just happened?

The pain, sight and smell of my own burnt flesh was still front and centre, but I started to think about what was going on. I remembered that I had been in a plane, that there were trees outside of my window; I remembered the crash and fire around me.

I started to look around, and recognized that I was in a thickly forested and rugged mountain area. There was a lot of smoke from a number of small fires burning throughout the trees. I walked toward the largest of the fires to see what I could find of the plane and the others. To the left of the wreckage site, a rock bluff went straight up approximately 20 metres high. A few metres to the right, a cliff went sharply down another 25 metres or so. The crash site was amongst trees half a metre in diameter. On the approach path to the crash site, there was a trail of fire and trees that all had their tops sheared off.

As soon as I saw the fractured burning wreckage of the passenger cabin amongst the rugged terrain, I knew that nobody else had survived the crash. I should not have been able to survive the crash. The horror of that moment has caused my subconscious to either block or erase that part of the video tape in my mind. I cannot remember anything I saw of the others, if anything. I just remember that I started to scream again. The emotion of the loss of my friends was crushing. I jumped around repeatedly, screaming "noooooo" at the top of my lungs.

I screamed and screamed again until I was out of strength to scream any more. Spent, drained and exhausted, I just stood there at the edge of the crash site crying uncontrollably. The loss of my friends and co-workers, and the insanity of the situation, was overwhelming. This was no bad dream, it was a living nightmare. I was hurt badly, cold, afraid and alone in the middle of a deserted forest.

This is what was left of the passenger cabin of the aircraft atop Thormanby Island. In the top left corner of the picture is the blue pontoon from the tip of the left wing. The centre area of the picture is the passenger cabin. The bottom right corner of the picture is where the right wing should be. The cockpit should be at the top right and the tail at the bottom left. The metal frame of my seat is visible in the middle of the picture.

Photo by crash investigation team

HOT AND COLD EMOTIONS

Struggling to mentally accept what had just happened, I started wandering around the crash site without purpose. I am not sure what I was even looking around for. The surrounding area was heavily forested, so in my condition I was restricted to travelling within the small clearing that had been made by the plane coming down. The fog was still thick, but I could see that I was on the side of a small mountain. I didn't have any idea where I was or, more importantly, where help was from here.

It was a good thing that I did not know how dire my situation was: that I was on uninhabited Thormanby Island, that Search and Rescue did not even know yet that we had gone down. Those facts might have caused me to give up hope entirely. Without this knowledge, I began a four-hour emotional roller coaster. I needed hope. I needed to keep believing that I was going to find help and survive. Only hope could help me find the strength to keep going.

The cold was becoming unbearable and I was shivering. In an attempt to keep warm, I moved closer to the flames of the burning wreckage. As I approached the heat, my hands and face felt like they were on fire again. I quickly opted to fight off the chill in the air rather than deal with more pain from my burns. Wanting to keep warm, yet that same warmth fuelling the pain of my burns, was a wry irony.

Still dazed and trying to figure out what to do, I noticed that there didn't seem to be a single sound coming from anywhere. Other than the sound of my own laboured breaths, the silence was deafening. It was eerie, and intensely lonely. Weeks later, I would learn that the foam earplugs I had put in before takeoff, the same earplugs that were mandatory for flight in the noisy aircraft, had been melted into my ear canals by the flames of my burning hoodie, robbing me of the sense of hearing.

The pain from my burns had not subsided, but my body and brain were quickly adapting to manage the pain enough to let me think as the amazing inherent will to survive welled up inside of me. I needed to form a survival plan. Without the use of my hands, I was incapable of creating shelter from the cold. The gash on my stomach was not bleeding badly, but without a mirror I could not fully evaluate my burns. In any event, I knew that I needed emergency treatment. When I summed everything up, the greatest immediate threat was hypothermia, followed by an intense desire for some kind of relief from the burn pain.

I knew that search and rescue teams would come looking for us, but I didn't think it would be soon, because they would not take the same risk of flying in the current foggy weather conditions. I decided that my best chance for survival was to leave the wreckage and look for help: a road, a cabin or maybe even a home with a phone. What I did not know was that the impact had been so forceful that the aircraft's emergency locator beacon was destroyed. No one knew yet that the plane had gone down or where we were.

With the decision to hike away from the crash site, I looked for the easiest route to hike down the mountain. As I started to move away from the wreckage, my conviction in this plan was tested early. Maneuvering down a steep mountain side, through thick underbrush, with badly burned hands and nothing to protect a burned torso from contact with trees, was a challenge. I knew this was not going to be easy, but I had to keep going. I had to keep my hope alive if I was going to get medical attention.

Hiking through the forest was a chess match; I would go a certain distance, and then stand in the trees to survey the path of least resistance ahead. I had to calculate not only where I would place my feet, but also how I was going to twist and turn my body through the branches to avoid any unnecessary contact. A tree branch touching any part of my skin felt like a searing brand. Minor scrapes were all accompanied by major screams.

About 15 minutes into my journey down the mountain, I came to a ledge at a steep angle with much steeper cliffs on either side. The ledge was the only option for going down; there was an immediate one metre drop, a narrow ledge, and then another two metre drop. Under normal circumstances, even a novice hiker would not consider this difficult to traverse. To me, this terrain was a substantial and very intimidating obstacle. Without the use of my hands, I calculated that I would have to sit on my butt, wiggle over the edge and do a controlled slide down to the ledge below. It was possible, but very risky. Falling the entire distance would not have killed me, but missing the first ledge and falling to the bottom would be a hard landing. Considering my severe injuries and sensitivity to touch, this was not a welcome thought.

I searched for other paths down, but the alternatives were all either thick forest or steeper drops. I was too far down the mountain to turn around and attempt climbing back up.

Raising burnt hands above my head, I squatted down and fell backward into a sitting position as gently as possible. I wriggled forward on the ground and swung my legs over the top of the ledge. Now positioned to start sliding down, I figured that I would lean forward or backward, using the position of my torso to control the fall. I slithered forward a bit more, began to slide down and leaned back to slow my descent. The entire length of my back scraped against the rocky ledge. I started to scream, and the debilitating panic came rushing back.

I landed on the ledge as planned, but in such agonizing pain and such a state of panic that I couldn't stand still. The idea of a controlled descent went out the window. I leaped off the ledge to get out of there. I tried to keep my knees bent to prepare for a soft landing, but I was now falling too quickly. When my feet hit the ground I had too much momentum and went into a hard forward roll. I raised my forearms over my face to try and protect myself, but I knew it was not going to be enough.

This was the first time I recall really focussing on the anticipation of the hurt that was coming my way as a result of my condition. It was not a pleasant feeling.

When I stopped rolling forward, I shot up immediately to stop making contact with anything. I jumped up and screamed to the point of exhaustion once again. I had conquered the obstacle, but at a nasty cost.

There was good news ahead. Below the ledge, the slope of the mountain became gentler and easier to navigate. Within a few minutes of hiking down, I came to a very shallow creek that was only a couple of metres wide. A new surge of hope ran through me. My first thought was that the creek would lead me to help. My logic was that people build things close to water, and I needed to believe that this creek would take me somewhere. If nothing else, it would lead me to the seashore. I was counting on it.

I stepped right into the middle of the creek and started to power-walk as fast as I could, no longer impeded by trees and branches. I remember thinking that this creek was my Autobahn as I tried to keep my thoughts focussed on progress rather than on the constant pain. I pushed with all of my might, and turned the power-walk into a light jog. I was exhausted, yet focussed on making progress as gently as my wounds would allow.

It was less than a kilometre before the small creek led to an inlet on the ocean. On the one hand I was happy to find the ocean, but I was also disappointed that I hadn't found any signs of civilization along the way. To have come this far and still be alone diminished some of the hope I had managed to gather up to this point.

Years after the crash, I learned the full trail of events that further delayed the start of the rescue operation for our crash.

Al "Bunny" Hailey and Fred Severre, two local hunters who were on Thormanby Island on November 16, 2008, heard what they felt was a plane crash and explosion, but they could not determine the exact location of the incident due to the poor visibility. Fred had a cell phone with him, and notified the local Royal Marine Search and Rescue Department, but the search and rescue team had not received any reports of a downed aircraft.

Our planned flight path was to take us to Powell River, BC, where we were to pick up one other passenger before continuing on to Toba Inlet.

When the plane was late for arrival at Powell River, the local charter representative called their dispatcher in Vancouver to determine the location of the plane using the aircraft's onboard GPS.

In the process of accessing the GPS location of the plane, the operator entered the previous day's date and time by mistake. On the previous day, the flight had bypassed Powell River, which is what the data showed. The Vancouver dispatcher assumed that the pilot had forgotten to go to Powell River and was still en route, heading directly for Toba Inlet.

Later, when the Toba Inlet charter representative also reported that the aircraft was late, it became obvious that something was wrong. The Vancouver dispatcher examined the GPS data again, but this time using the correct date, and realized that something was indeed wrong. Dispatch notified central search and rescue, who had previously received the report of a plane crash from Fred. With all of these corresponding pieces of information, the official rescue operation began.

ALONE AT THE SEA OF DESPAIR

The creek drained out through an inlet at the apex of a cove on the ocean. Walking down to the sea, I saw a yellow tarp washed up onto the shore. My first thought was to use the tarp to increase my visibility, but then I thought about wrapping myself in the tarp to protect myself from the ocean breeze and keep warm. As I approached the tarp, I tried to develop a plan to somehow do both without the use of my hands.

Standing on the shore, I was still scanning the horizon for a boat or any sign of help. To my left was thick forest atop steep cliffs. To the right the inlet was lined by a shallow cliff leading out to a large peninsula of large boulders. A plan started coming together; I would make a jacket out of this tarp and then make my way out to the tip of the peninsula, where surely I would be visible to someone in the area. Hope of survival welled up again.

I moved to the shore, and used my feet to spread the tarp out on the rocks. My plan was to use my steel-toed work boots to kick arm and head holes in the fabric. Then I figured I could kick the tarp back toward the trees and high enough to get my arms and head through the holes.

I got the tarp flattened out easily enough, but kicking a hole in a tarp turned out to be more difficult than I had hoped – it was in better shape and tougher to penetrate than anticipated. After repeatedly kicking at the tarp without success, I got very angry. The thought of having this unlikely gift dropped in my lap, figuring out a plan to use it for survival, and then not being physically able to do it, was frustrating.

Intense frustration can be a powerful feeling. I started kicking furiously at the tarp in a rage, as though it was responsible for everything that had taken place that day. There was so much emotion inside of me. I was scared, grieving for my friends, and in a brutal amount of pain. I flailed at the tarp to the point of exhaustion. Once again, when my fit came to an end, I started crying uncontrollably. Damn it! I had come so far but still struggling to fend off the fear that I was going to die. I just needed to stand there and cry for a little while.

Once I calmed down a bit, I focussed my anger on the tarp. I used my feet to position it against sharper rocks. This time, I placed my kicks strategically. The tarp began to yield, and I was able to kick out two armholes where I needed them.

With my energy waning, I gave up on the idea of creating a third hole for my head to form a poncho-like jacket. Instead, I slid the tarp along the ground with my feet and then kicked it up into the shoreline trees, high enough to get my arms through. Facing the trees, I gently pushed my hands through the holes in the tarp and raised my arms up over my head. The tarp slid down onto my forearms and dangled in front of me. It was quite large, so the extra material trailed out between my legs, making it difficult to walk, but wrapped in the tarp, I could feel instant relief from the stinging salty breeze blowing in from the ocean.

My best chance for being seen was to get out onto the far tip of the peninsula. There was a narrow cliff-like passage leading out along the right side of the peninsula, but the drop from it was straight down into the ocean. The thought of falling into the water commanded fear. It looked risky, but I had no other choice.

The peninsula was formed by large boulders left over from the ice age surrounded by sea logs washed ashore. The tarp was clumsy and made it difficult to move; half wearing, half dragging the makeshift jacket, I started to pick my way toward the rocky outcrop jutting out into the ocean. I gingerly balanced my way out across wet and slippery rocks. In the event of a fall, I would not be able to use my hands to catch myself. All movements were calculated, slow and cautious.

I made it across the ledge and stood at the base of the peninsula. I would have to make short leaps from boulder to boulder to get to the tip. On the third leap, I lost my footing on the slippery rocks and came crashing down. My hands slapped against the rocks as I fell. The pain was instantly excruciating. I just laid there and screamed. Every time I reinjured my burns, it was as sharp and debilitating, both physically and mentally. After calming down, I twisted my body around, using my elbows and knees to find a way back to my feet without using my hands.

Little by little, the fog started to lift, offering greater visibility. Across the bay from the peninsula I could begin to make out houses among the trees and boats floating in the harbour! Another rush of hope filled my body with energy and excitement. I was sure that I would be seen and rescued now. As soon as I could get someone to see me, the countdown to the end of this nightmare would begin.

I looked across the bay to the houses on the other side, then jumped frantically and waved my arms in an attempt to get someone's attention. I started screaming "hey" and "help" with everything I had. On the one hand I knew it was too far for anyone to hear me, but it didn't matter. It felt good to scream anyway.

The wind out on the peninsula blew in from the ocean in a strong and steady manner. The cold, salty sea breeze stung my burns. With the rush of excitement for quick rescue wearing off after a few minutes, the cold wind became too much to bear. As hope ebbed, I needed a break to retrench. Getting out of the wind meant a trip back to the cover of the trees for some relief. I very carefully picked my way back across the boulders and took refuge in the bush on the shoreline.

Resting in the lee of the trees, I kept wishing for the comfort of a hospital and the thought of being put to sleep with pain-relieving drugs. The unrelenting pain from the burns was starting to wear on my ability to fight. I was SO close to help. I convinced myself that someone would see me. I was draped in a big bright yellow tarp on the rocks of an island. I believed that standing out on the rocks and waving my arms would eventually get someone's attention. Who knew, maybe even a ship would come by. With my hope recharged, I headed back into the biting wind on the peninsula. Again, step by step, very carefully out across the dangerous rocks.

In addition to the foam earplugs melted into my ears robbing me of the sense of hearing, I had lost my eyeglasses in the plane crash, making sight a challenge. As I peered across the bay toward the boats and houses in search of detail, I began to realize just how far away they were. I waved my arms in the air again, but this time with much less passion and enthusiasm. Soon my arms got tired from waving, and I just stood there silently, hoping and praying.

It was not long before the cold wind forced me back to the shelter of the shore again. I made four trips from the shelter of the trees across the slippery rocks to the tip of the peninsula. Each time staying as long as I could bear and waving as much as I could. My ability to fight off the cold was weakening along with my hope. I didn't think I would be able to survive much longer if I wasn't found.

Hiding in the trees from the wind after my fourth trip, I decided that I would not make another. I started to question my decision to leave the crash site. I thought that if I could get back up the cliff that I could get close enough to a fire to keep warm and wait for a search and rescue team to arrive.

Desperate to find warmth, I decided to try and make my way back up the mountain. As I turned back toward the creek, I admitted to myself that I had absolutely no chance of getting back up the ledge that I had tumbled down earlier. I also knew I couldn't just sit in the trees by the ocean any longer. I had to do something. I had to hang onto hope of some kind, some plan for my rescue, some way of not dying alone on this shore.

The walk up the bed of the creek was slow and lethargic. Everything was becoming a chore. I felt like I would not be able to keep up this physical and emotional battle much longer. Slowly moving forward along the creek, under the thick canopy of the forest, a faint noise started to get my attention. At first

I couldn't make it out, but it started getting louder. It was the distinct sound of a helicopter. I couldn't believe it. This was the best thing ever! I was saved!

I frantically looked for a clearing to somehow signal the helicopter, but I was back under the thick canopy of forest. The helicopter would not be able to see me unless I could get into the open. I couldn't believe it! The sound became a little louder. Then, as I desperately looked through the trees to see if I could figure out where it was coming from, the sound started to fade.

Almost as soon as it had started, the sound of the helicopter faded into the distance.

Despite this blow, I wasn't going to give up. I thought that the helicopter might pass by the coast. Hanging onto my last bit of hope, I turned and started to jog back down the creek again. As I was making my way back to the inlet, a new emotion crept in: I could feel rage rising up in me. After all that I had endured today, and within a mere 15 minutes of leaving the rocks, a helicopter came by and then left! I knew the helicopter would have seen me if I would have stayed back there. Why? Why?? I started to feel like God was working against me. I needed this madness to stop.

When I made it back to where the creek met the ocean, I didn't see any signs of rescue. No boats. No sound of engines. Once again I was standing there at the sea, still alone and in unbearable pain. It was at that point that I lost it.

I was consumed with rage and anger. I started pointing my finger to the sky and began yelling, "WHY!!!?"

As tears of grief and defeat streamed down my face, I screamed at God and demanded an answer.

"Why!!!? Why did you burn me?" I screamed. "Why did you make me live, burn me, make me endure all that I have today, only to take my life on this shore anyway?"

I remember that moment very clearly. I gave up hope. I was ready to die.

The acceptance of defeat and death was very lonely. I remember that I felt more alone at that second in my life than I ever had before. I would have given everything I had, or ever would have, just to tell the people in my life that I loved how much they really meant to me before I died.

I was mad about being burnt, but I was now okay with dying; I had had enough of the pain.

BACK ACROSS THE WATER AND INTO THE ARMS OF SALVATION

Fate was playing a twisted game with me that day. Standing alone on the shore, after accepting defeat and death, I heard something.

From the silence and loneliness came the faint sound of an engine. It was not a helicopter, but it was getting louder.

Suddenly a red Zodiac boat came around the cliffs on the left side of the inlet. I started waving and screaming again, and the boat headed directly toward me!

I was so excited that I tried to wade out into the ocean toward the boat, but the icy saltwater stung the burns on my legs so sharply that I could not get any further than up to my knees. When the Zodiac got a bit closer, one of the rescuers yelled to me and asked if I was in a plane crash. I replied back that yes, I was. Next he asked if anyone else was alive. I dropped my head and simply replied, "No one but me." It was the first time that I had said the words out loud, and they were hard to utter.

With my emotions churning, I broke the silence sharply and yelled to the rescuers to ask what time it was. This took them a little off-guard, but a man replied that it was 3 p.m. I angrily yelled back at him, "What took you so fucking long!?" I was a little surprised at myself for saying that, but I was an angry and emotional mess at this point.

As the boat drew near to shore and the rescue team saw the extent of my burns, I could hear them discussing how they were going to lift me into the boat. Two of them leaned over the side, grabbed my forearms well above my burnt hands, and pulled me out of the water to the side of the boat. Then one of them (Bob) grabbed my belt, hauled me completely on board, and gently put me down on the floor of the bow. He immediately started covering me with blankets while his partner rushed to the controls to get the boat heading back to the mainland.

My battle for the moment was at an end. I was in a coast-guard boat on the way to a hospital.

I was rescued.

A feeling of relief came over me like no other I have ever experienced. Only ten minutes earlier, I had given up hope and genuinely believed that my life was at an end. To have it given back this way created intense feelings that are hard to describe. I was filled with gratitude for being rescued, for simply being alive. I was more thankful for life than I had ever imagined before. I vowed that I would never undervalue life again.

With our small boat now turned back out to sea, Bob gave the thumbs-up to his partner and the boat accelerated sharply. Just as the Grumman Goose had pounded across the top of the waves during takeoff, I was once again bouncing across the sea, this time in the opposite direction.

The pounding waves and the roar of the boat engine made it difficult to communicate, but Bob told me that my saviours were with the Royal Canadian Marine Search and Rescue team – the volunteer coast guard from the nearby town of Sechelt. He said there was a large search going on, but the plane hadn't been located yet. I described the creek, the cliff, and the path back up the mountain to the crash site. Then he told me to relax and stay covered up, that we would be at the mainland soon.

As I lay there at the bottom of that boat, I started thinking about my family. I didn't know what they knew, or even if they knew anything at all. I started getting very emotional, and urging Bob to call my sister. I wanted someone to call my family to let them know what had happened. He promised that someone would contact them soon.

Thankfully, it only took a few minutes to reach the dock on the mainland. I was anxiously anticipating medical help. The boat started slowing down as we approached a large pier lined with emergency vehicles: police cars, ambulances and fire trucks all with their lights on stood at the ready. I could also see news vans, reporters, and what appeared to be a small gathering of onlookers. It was humbling to see that so many people cared about us.

Below the large pier was a smaller wooden dock with a ramp that led up to the main dock, where all of the emergency vehicles were parked. As we approached the smaller wooden dock, I saw two paramedics standing ready with a stretcher. The Zodiac came alongside the dock, and before we were secure, the paramedics jumped into the boat.

I was trying to get up. I wanted to get out of the boat on my own, but the paramedics would have none of that. They insisted I remain still and they would put me on the stretcher. They worked very quickly, and had me on the stretcher in no time. Within a few seconds, I was strapped in and being carried up the ramp to the main pier where the stretcher was quickly put into a waiting ambulance. As the doors shut, I could see people trying to approach us. The paramedics had put me in the ambulance quickly, but it was apparent there was also some media commotion on the pier.

I had been anticipating this moment for so long that it was very emotional. I started to get worked up again, and relentlessly asked the paramedic to call my family. She promised to do so. And then came some bad news. She told me that they weren't expecting burn victims, and that she didn't have a licence to deliver painkillers. Was some dark force somewhere conspiring to keep me in this agony?

The paramedic immediately radioed another ambulance to arrange for an attendant that could administer injections. The second ambulance set out from the opposite direction to meet us halfway to the hospital. I began to sob. Again, some of it was the pain, but there was so much more than that. Everything was overwhelming and emotional. I had been in pain for so long now that all I wanted was for it to finally stop.

With sirens blaring and lights flashing, we tore off toward the local hospital. The paramedic asked if I knew my name and if I remembered what had happened. I could tell that she was trying to keep my mind occupied while she started to assess my wounds. As we travelled, she cut off my jeans and boots. She kept asking if it hurt anywhere else, but that was difficult to answer – it hurt everywhere. She seemed concerned about broken bones and internal injuries. I assured her that I was fine, and that burns were my only issue.

Suddenly the ambulance braked hard and pulled over to the side of the road. A moment later, the back doors burst open and another paramedic jumped in. Just as quickly, the doors were shut and we started rolling again. The new paramedic began getting a needle ready. I have always hated needles, but I was not afraid of this one. I couldn't wait for this one. I know that at this point I must have still been in shock and running on adrenaline, but despite these two natural protectors, the level of pain was still overwhelming. For the first time in the more-than four hours since I had been on fire, I was finally going to get some relief. The paramedic gave me the needle, and then the two of them went back to assessing my wounds, engaging me in small chat the entire time.

Again I started insisting that someone call my sister Isobel. The first paramedic stopped what she was doing and took the time to write down Isobel's name and phone number. She promised me that she would call. My emotions were all over the place, my mind was racing, reflecting on the day, thinking of everything that had happened. Trying to keep myself rational was difficult to do.

As soon as we arrived at the hospital, I was rushed from the ambulance into a room where a doctor and nurses were waiting. I expected them to start doing some kind of work on me, but to my surprise they didn't. The medical team tried to comfort me, took my vital signs, and gave me another injection for the pain. The doctor informed me that an air ambulance helicopter was already on its way to take me to Vancouver General Hospital where they were better equipped to deal with burns. Thankfully, the injection from the doctor took me to the edge of consciousness. I fell asleep.

When I woke up, I was again strapped to a stretcher and being bounced around a little. As I opened my eyes and tried to focus, I could see that everyone was wearing shiny helmets and uniforms. I was being unloaded from a helicopter. I looked around, still in a haze from being heavily sedated. It was dark now. I could see the lights from the tops of the buildings surrounding the hospital.

I remember feeling disappointed; I had never been in a helicopter before and had just missed an amazing view of the city lights of Vancouver. I was now in what seemed to be a dream, dangling at the edge of consciousness, drifting in and out of a drug-induced haze.

The next time I woke up, I was in a room in the intensive-care wing of the hospital. My wounds had still not been tended to. Dead, burnt skin was still hanging from various parts of my body. My hands and face were swollen. I was dirty from the mountain hike and still reeked of smoke, burnt hair and flesh. I was confused about my dirty condition.

A nurse came into the room as soon as I woke up. She told me that I was at Vancouver General Hospital and that my sister Isobel was on her way. I was groggy from the drugs, and found it very difficult to focus and communicate. The pain was still there but seemed to be on the outer edge of consciousness, not demanding my full attention now.

The first thing I said to the nurse was that everyone else was dead. Now that I was in medical care, my mind and heart were free to think about the lives that were lost that day. I had just lived through it hours ago; all of those men had just died and I was there with them. I had had breakfast with my two friends just before they died. It had all happened so quickly, and now their lives were over. My heart was heavy with grief for my friends and co-workers; I needed to release my sadness. I just lay there sobbing to myself.

Later that evening, I started to think about what the next few months would hold. I knew that my battle was not over, and that it had only changed from survival to recovery. Little did I realize that the hardest battle of my life was about to begin.

A couple of hours later, the nurse came in and told me that my sister had arrived. Isobel walked in right behind her and went directly to the foot of my bed. As soon as she put her hand on my leg I burst out crying uncontrollably and started hyperventilating. The nurse and Isobel both came to my side and tried to calm me down, telling me that it was okay and that I needed to slow down and breathe. They kept repeating that everything was going to be all right. I just needed to cry and let it out. As Isobel stood at the side of my bed, we both had rivers of tears streaming down our faces.

Isobel told me that the rest of the family was on their way from Alberta to Vancouver, and that they would be at the hospital in the morning. That was very good news. She went on to tell me that because of the media coverage, the hospital had set up security to keep the media out and give me privacy. A password was required to get past security, and my family was in control of the password. The hospital even went as far as to keep my name off their official patient list. The tragic crash, and my survival, had become a top national news story.

The news of the tragedy travelled quickly through Kiewit. The next day, a few of my close friends from work would make the trip to Vancouver to see me. These people were more like family than co-workers or friends. We were like brothers.

Isobel stayed at the hospital all day Monday, controlling the password. She knew that I would be happy to see co-workers who made the trek to see me. My closest friend, Doug, walked past my room because he didn't recognize me. My face was so swollen and burnt that my best friend couldn't even recognize me. When he realized his mistake and came into the room, I started to cry uncontrollably with grief once more. It was terrible to be so emotional every time that I saw someone for the first time, but it was not in my control. Releasing the grief through tears helped me. My visitors didn't stay long; it was hard for anyone to find the right words. To have them visit was enough.

The same thing happened when my father arrived. My brother Mike and my father (Tom Sr.) drove 12 hours through the Rocky Mountains to get to the hospital in Vancouver. They arrived on Monday, November 17, my father's birthday. When he came into my room, I could see on his face that his heart was broken. It hurt him to see his son in such bad condition and in so much pain, but he was so thankful that he didn't lose his son, as others had. I know that he would have taken my place if he could have. It was great to see Mike as well. He would play an important role over the next few days, and in the rest of my recovery.

When my mother, Isa, flew in on Monday afternoon, the family was all reunited. What I saw in her eyes when she first saw me in such a condition was similar to what I had seen in my father's. We also shared an emotional moment together.

I remained dirty and in intensive care, going in and out of sedated consciousness. I had no idea what lay in store for me the next day. The ignorance of not knowing was a blessing.

CLEANSED AT LAST

On Tuesday, I learned that the doctors had confirmed that I did not have any broken bones or internal injuries. Following this good news, a number of nurses came into my room and told me that it was time to properly clean my wounds and begin the skin-healing process.

To do so, they would have to submerse me in a chemical cleansing bath. As if the thought of being submersed in a bath wasn't painful enough, they continued to tell me they would have to scrub my wounds. The purpose of the scrub was to remove the dead skin and any debris embedded in my body. They were going to thoroughly scrub my burnt flesh and it was going to be the most painful experience imaginable.

My heart immediately started pounding, and my eyes welled up with tears. I literally couldn't handle the thought of my hands or face being scrubbed in a bath. The panic returned; anxiety and terrible anticipation took over my mind. My heart started racing and my breathing became heavy. I began uncontrollably squirming at the thought – this was like being told that they were going to light me on fire again. I honestly didn't believe I had it in me to bear that kind of pain once more. It felt like I was losing my mind with the anticipation as they prepared to take me to the bath in the next room.

I begged and pleaded with them to put me to sleep. If it had to be done, I wanted to be put under for it. I could see they felt bad for me and empathized with how I was feeling. They told me that I had to be awake when I was put into the bath as it had something to do with the shock. The anticipation was almost as bad as what was coming, and only made everything seem worse.

The nurses assisted me into the room where the torturous bath would take place. I was crying and begging and pleading the whole way. The nurses looked close to tears with empathy for me. I was almost at the point of losing my mind, right beside the tub. As they started to position me into the bath, everything went dark.

Blessed merciful darkness.

Of all the things that I went through relating to the plane crash, aside from being momentarily knocked unconscious at the moment of impact, that bath was the only other event that drove me to lose consciousness. I don't know if I passed out from the pain and shock of hitting the bath, or if it was a mental shutdown forced by my brain. I am not even sure I care why I passed out; I am just thankful that I did. What I was going through was torture; the thought of them scrubbing my burns and wounds was unimaginable. I don't know how any human could stay awake through that kind of physical pain and mental anxiety. It was too much for me.

When I regained consciousness again, I could feel a fresh tingling of pain coming from my wounds. There wasn't any more pain than before the bath, but it was a different feeling.

While I was still unconscious, the nurses had dressed all of my wounds. My fingers were wrapped individually. My hands were bandaged. My entire head, my stomach and parts of my legs were bandaged. While that bath had been the worst experience imaginable, I was happy to see that my wounds were cleaned and bandaged at last.

Now that the bath and the dressing of my wounds was complete, there was not a lot that could be done for me. I was left to lie in a bed, and given time for my flesh to heal. Having family close made all the difference in the world as I began to wrestle with the emotional scars that would outlast the burn scars.

Tom in the intensive care unit. Photo by Michael Wilson
My right thigh burned by the plane fuel soaking through my jeans.
Photo by the University of Alberta

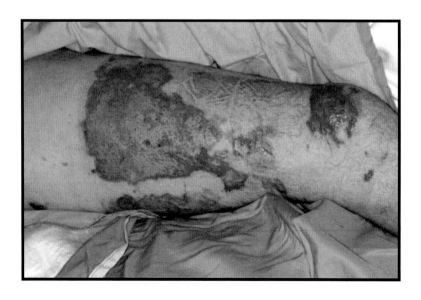

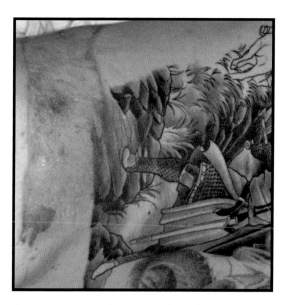

My left side and my back. These burns are from the seatbelt where the fire was able to get past clothing

Photo by the University of Alberta

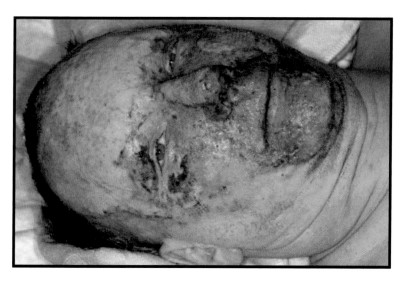

My forehead was one of the worst burnt parts of my body. The doctors were considering skin grafts of my forehead. My neck is still very swollen three days later.

Photo by the University of Alberta

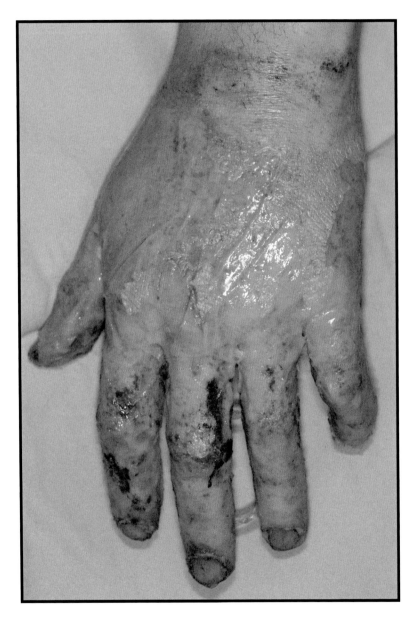

The back of my left hand. There is a large amount of plasma.
Photo by the University of Alberta

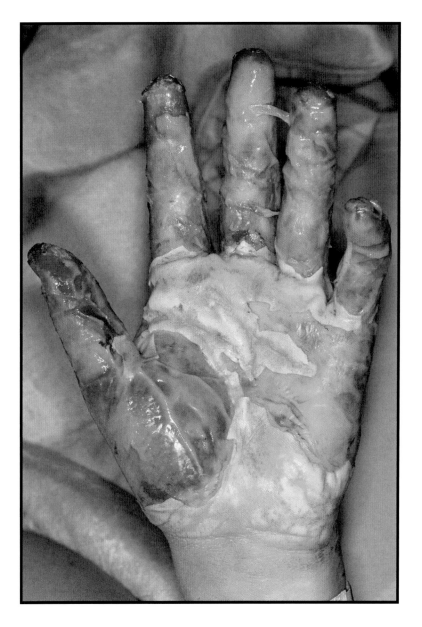

The palm of my hand. You can see he plasma stuck between my fingers.
Photo by the University of Alberta.

ANGELS AND NIGHTMARES

The human body cannot typically withstand the kind of deceleration forces that I had experienced during the crash. The doctors were puzzled by my lack of internal injuries or broken bones. I had escaped with only a few cuts and multiple burns.

During the first few days in the hospital, I remained heavily drugged, and moved in and out of consciousness. At least my family was close by while I was awake.

There was not much that the doctors could do to assist the healing process at this point. I needed to remain in intensive care to give my body time to settle down and reduce swelling before I could be transferred to a burn unit for the next phase of recovery.

I was on an emotional roller coaster, and the pain made it difficult to control my mood. At the peaks I felt strength and commitment to fight through this. The valleys of the roller coaster were full of self-pity, despair and sorrow. My pain and my emotions also made it difficult to concentrate on things going on around me; my family did what they could to keep me informed. They also assured me that they were there for me when I was ready to talk, but I was nowhere near being able to speak about any of the details of the crash or what I had gone through.

The crash had become front-page news, and by now my whereabouts had leaked out. On Tuesday afternoon, a media conference was set up at the hospital. Dr. John Reid and my brother Mike both agreed to speak. Dr. Reid described my survival, without broken bones or internal injuries, as remarkable. Mike told the reporters that I was not ready to talk to anyone yet about the ordeal, and asked the press for privacy.

That evening, I asked to watch the news to see my brother on TV. I don't know what I was expecting from the newscasts, but I quickly became upset at the way the story was being told. My thoughts were with my lost friends and co-workers. While the news story did briefly mention the deaths of the other passengers, the main focus was on the unlikeliness of my survival. The whole thing had a sensationalism to it that I had not anticipated. I resented it.

Later that night, after visiting hours were over, my emotions were still churning as I tried to get some sleep. The constant pain made it difficult, but the drugs helped.

That was the night the nightmare began.

I dreamt that I was stuck in the basement of my sister's house and the house was on fire.

I could see the flames coming closer and closer to me, but I couldn't fit my body through the small basement window to escape. The anticipation of being burned alive was horrifying. I became so panicked in my dream that I woke up terrified.

The dream would recur almost nightly for weeks to come. My mind was having difficulty letting go of the shock of regaining consciousness at the crash site and being on fire. It would take time and healing before I would no longer have nightmares about burning alive. The days were long and physically painful; the nights were long and painful in my mind.

On Wednesday morning, as my family arrived at the hospital, they were met by a small team of investigators from the Transportation Safety Board. The investigators requested some time to interview me. I knew that this interview was important, even though I wasn't mentally ready to talk about the crash yet. As the only survivor, I had a responsibility to help them piece together what had happened.

I recognized the lead investigator as one of the people who had been on the TV news story the previous evening. Fortunately, the investigators did not ask any questions about what happened after the crash; they were only concerned about the events that had led up to the incident. They asked if I had heard or seen any signs of the plane malfunctioning or if I had any idea what had caused the crash to happen. I told them everything that I have told you about the minutes before the crash, including that the pilot gave us the opportunity to get off the plane. I told them how fast it happened, and that it was over in just a few seconds. I said I believed we had lost our way in the dense fog, were off course and flew into the side of the mountain because the pilot couldn't see it. It was that simple.

The investigators were very kind, and didn't push me too hard with their questions. Their compassion was a welcome contrast to how the media had reported the story the previous evening.

Before they left, the lead investigator looked me in the eyes and told me that in his 30 years of aircraft crash investigations he had never seen anyone walk away from a wreckage like that. He said that there must have been an angel with me, and a special reason that I was alive.

The investigator's comment caught me off guard. If indeed an angel had been there with me, I prayed that the angel would help guide me through my recovery as well.

Oddly enough, one of my wounds that required stitches is in the shape of a hook. In the days ahead, as I started to share more of my story with family, we mused that the angel must have used a hook to pull me from death and save me that day.

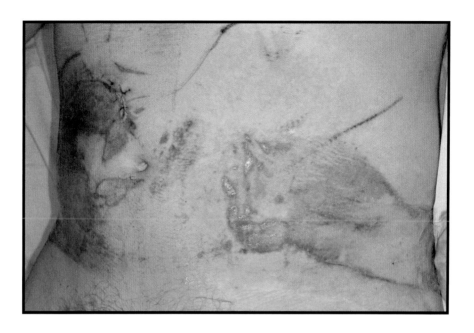

This is a picture of my stomach. On the top left is the "angel's hook".
Photo by the University of Alberta

I did feel that I survived for a reason; there was something to learn from it. I had no idea how anything good could possibly come out of that day, but if it could, I was determined to find it. The investigator had sparked my will to fight through this. I was blessed to still be alive. I had been given a gift, and even if I didn't understand why, I was not going to let that gift go to waste.

CLOSER TO HOME

The media started following my brother Mike back and forth from the hospital to his hotel and pestering him with questions. The rest of my family learned to walk separately to avoid being identified. Reporters also went to my brother's house and also started contacting my friends. The hospital stepped up security to keep reporters from reaching my room.

I knew that people were concerned for me and wanted to know more, but I was not ready yet. They knew that I was alive and that needed to be enough for now. I wasn't ready to let people see me burnt. I didn't want to answer any questions; I just wanted to grieve alone with my family.

I did feel a need to communicate with the families of those lost and with the people at work. They were grieving the loss of their friends and loved ones as well. It was a sad time for everyone. I couldn't imagine how sad it was for the families affected the most by this tragedy. My sister Isobel became my liaison with Kiewit co-workers. The company gave my family a great deal of respect and compassion throughout this entire experience, and it will always be appreciated. Kiewit offered to help in any way they could. It was nice to know that they were there to help if we needed them.

My father was beside himself, seeing me in my condition. There was nothing that he could do to help me, which made him very restless. We came up with a plan to send him out for Slurpees (an ice-slush drink) from a local convenience store. I wasn't allowed to eat solid food yet, and the cold drink felt good on my throat. Each trip to the store would take my dad a half -hour or so, and over the next month he would bring me several Slurpees a day. It kept him busy and feeling like he was doing something helpful, which he was.

Day by day I continued to regain strength, but we all knew that I was going to be hospitalized for some time yet. It was not practical for me to remain in a hospital in Vancouver a thousand kilometres from home. I needed my family to provide ongoing support, but they had jobs and lives to get back to as well. I needed to be moved to an Edmonton-area hospital.

Fortunately, there is an excellent burn unit at the University of Alberta Hospital in Edmonton, and the doctors in Vancouver agreed to release me from the intensive care unit so that I could be moved. The next challenge was finding a way to get me to Edmonton. The hospital staff proposed booking a ticket on a commercial flight, but informed us that they would not be able to send medical supervision to accompany me. Needless to say, this was not a welcome idea. I was concerned about flying in general and about the possibility of getting in medical distress along the way. We were all concerned about the difficulty of trying to move me through a public airport in my condition. With all of my bandages I looked like a mummy, so there was also concern about the possibility of creating a media circus and being bombarded with questions that I wasn't ready to answer.

When Isobel described our travel dilemma to the folks at Kiewit the company promptly arranged for one of their private jets to transport me from Vancouver to Edmonton. This kind and generous offer brought a lot of relief to all of us.

The next morning, everyone gathered in my room early. My father and brother had driven to Vancouver earlier in the week and needed to take their car back to Edmonton. They departed first to begin the 12-hour journey home. Soon after, an ambulance arrived to take my mother, Isobel and me to the airport.

As I was being wheeled from my room to the ambulance, I asked the nurse if we could stop for a cigarette. It had been several days since I had had a smoke. I was going to get my sister to hold it for me. Before the nurse could respond, Isobel said, "Tom, you are still smoking from the crash. You don't need a cigarette."

We both started to laugh. The nurse didn't know what to say, but this was the first time I had laughed since the crash, and it felt good. My mom didn't think it was that funny, but we did. It was good to start this difficult trip on a lighter note. We were on our way home.

WELCOME TO THE BURN WARD

The ambulance trip was uneventful, which was a good thing because I was trying to mentally prepare myself to get back on another plane. My mother saw that I was struggling with this; she sat beside me and reassured me the entire way. It doesn't matter how old you are, when you are hurt and scared, there is nothing quite like comforting from your mom.

Approaching the Vancouver airport, the ambulance turned through a secure set of gates to the executive airstrip and then right out onto the tarmac. We pulled up alongside Kiewit's corporate jet. Standing at the bottom of the stairs to the plane, waiting to greet us, was Dick Colf, a Kiewit vice president. Dick is a true gentleman, with a good sense of humour and a great heart. As we boarded the jet and prepared for takeoff, he asked if I was going to be okay with flying. Surprisingly I was; this sleek and modern jet with sophisticated instrumentation put me at ease. I was ready to go home.

Dick didn't ask too many details about the crash. After a few minutes, he began regalling my mom with some of his personal stories. He had a way of making people smile, and kept the mood light the entire way. Before we knew it, we were on the ground again in Edmonton, where another ambulance was waiting on the tarmac to rush us to the U of A hospital. Since I was in stable condition, I would have thought that we would have taken our time, but with the ambulance lights flashing and sirens blaring we made it to the hospital in very good time.

In the intensive care unit of the Vancouver hospital I had been kept drugged while my body did some early recovery. My bandages had not been changed since they were applied right after my bath. I was looking forward to being in this U of A hospital with a ward dedicated to burn treatment.

Day One

The hospital was expecting us; I was checked in at the emergency department and taken to the burn ward immediately. My mother had ridden with me in the ambulance, but was asked to stay behind at this point as the doctors wanted to do an immediate and thorough assessment of my condition.

There are secure double doors leading into the burn ward and a large sign that says "restricted access". A security camera and badge access controlled the door; I was very thankful for the privacy that they provided. Behind the doors, there is a large nursing station in the centre with hallways leading off in either direction. I noticed that the hallways were lined with large glass windows.

As I was wheeled to my room at the end of the hallway, I could see through the glass windows, into the rooms of the other burn-unit patients. Each room was quite large and had only one patient in it. The glass windows were obviously used to monitor patients without having to enter the room. Each room has a separate small anteroom at the entrance for all visitors to scrub and gown before entering to reduce the chance of patient infections. Scrubbing, putting on a mask, gloves and hospital gown were all conditions of being able to see me in the days ahead.

Once inside my room, one of the doctors explained what would happen next. The nurses were going to remove all of the bandages and dressings from my body. The doctors would then assess each burned area, and have a photographer take a picture of each one (these are the photographs that I shared with you earlier in the book).

At first I was interested in this. I hadn't seen my burns since they had been cleaned, and I was curious to see how they looked.

The nurses explained that since my bandages had not been removed in a few days they were likely stuck to my wounds. This meant that the removal process was going to be painful. I could immediately feel my body start to squirm in anticipation of this procedure. The emotional stress of knowing what was coming was the hardest thing to go through again and again.

The nurses were very soft and reassuring. I was given a fresh shot of morphine, and they proceeded to start unwrapping me. I think there were three or four nurses working at once to try and get this done as quickly as possible. As they unwrapped the bandages and the layers got closer to my burns, it brought all of the pain and panic back full-throttle.

As soon as I began to squirm and scream, the nurses worked faster to get me through this as quickly as possible, and kept reassuring me that they were almost done. Once the last bandage was off, they all backed away and gave me a little time to breathe. Time to regain control of my emotions. Despite being in a great deal of pain, the fresh air against my exposed wounds felt oddly good. The fresh air felt crisp, clean, and even though painful, it was a different kind of pain.

I started to calm down and stop squirming; the doctors asked me to move around into different positions so they could take pictures and assess the severity of each burn individually. Although moving around into various positions was uncomfortable, the un-bandaging was over.

My body started to generate a large amount of clear plasma. This plasma assists wounds in healing. The plasma covered large areas of my hands and face. I did not get to see any of the pictures until after I was released from the hospital; I could see my hands, stomach and legs but not my back or my face. The plasma was strung between my fingers. Out of curiosity I tried to wiggle my fingers. The pain was immediate and unforgiving. I would not attempt that again for a while.

The doctors did not say much. They completed their initial assessment, and said they would return the next morning to discuss my burns and recovery plan in more detail. The nurses gave me a few minutes alone to relax before coming back in to re-wrap each of my wounds. On the one hand, I felt better about this place; the doctors and nurses were all specialists and experienced at treating burns. On the other hand, I began feeling sorry for myself. I had a feeling that this was going to be a very difficult place to exist; the treatment necessary to heal me was going to be a form of torture.

My mother and sister stayed at the hospital and spent a little time with me that evening, but they hadn't been home in a while so the visit was short. My dad and brother were still on the road doing the long drive from Vancouver back to Edmonton and wouldn't arrive home until late that night.

The first evening was very quiet. It was the first time I had been given some time to myself. Assessing the situation, I began to grasp my complete state of dependence. My life was reduced from being a busy, successful business manager to being confined to a bed. There was no thought of meetings, schedules, goals or money. I couldn't get out of bed. I couldn't change the channel on the TV. I couldn't hold a glass of water or feed myself. Worst of all, I couldn't clean or take care of myself in any way. I felt humiliated; to have to rely on others for the most basic and private of things was a very difficult thing to accept. My entire existence was about getting from one moment to the next, and at this point I had no idea how long I was going to be like this.

The bed was equipped with a big red foot-button that allowed me to inject morphine into my intravenous drip at will, within certain limits. Morphine brought temporary escape, but also robbed me of the ability to think clearly. I pushed the button and kept my morphine drip running at maximum capacity for the entire night – as much to reduce my mental anguish as the physical pain.

I had been looking forward to getting to a burn ward to start a specific healing program. Now the depressing reality of the tough road ahead set in. I remember lying there, wallowing in self-pity, fading in and out of consciousness all night, thinking to myself, "Welcome to the burn ward."

THE SEARCH FOR MEANING

After that first night in the burn ward, I gave myself a stern talking-to. I had to lose the self-pity. I committed to becoming a better person. I became, and still am, convinced that there was somehow something important to be learned from my experience. As tragic as the crash and loss of lives was, I decided that it was going to be equally tragic if I failed to make some meaning of it and grow from it. I clung to this conviction, and it gave me something to focus on throughout my recovery.

The pain was relentless. If you can imagine a time when you might have burned a finger or forearm on a hot stove or toaster, and then amplify that level of pain by a thousand times or more, you will get a sense of what I was feeling. Burns are unlike the pain from a cut or a broken bone; the pain associated with these types of injuries gradually subsides. We can often find a comfortable position with a bruise or cut and, if we are careful not to move, the pain subsides temporarily. The pain from burns does not decrease in intensity from hour to hour. There is no such thing as a comfortable position to lie in that will alleviate the pain – it is on high level all the time.

I hated every second of it, but there was nothing that I could do except decide to accept it and try to find a way to fight through it.

In the days ahead, there were a number of moments of impact in the burn ward that I specifically remember for the manner in which they affected me. Every moment served a different purpose in my search for meaning.

THE DAILY ROUTINE

Day Two

The burn ward marches to a pretty strict schedule for things like visiting hours, meals and bandage changes. Each patient in the ward needs a great deal of care and attention, so keeping things on a strict schedule is important to maintain order.

I remember meeting the day-shift nurse who came in early the next morning. I liked her right away. The nurses in the burn ward were amazingly gentle, caring, and compassionate people. They would patiently listen to all of my questions and do their best to answer them. Although my experience in the burn ward was terrible, the people that helped me through it are a part of my experience that I cherish.

I started to question the day nurse about my recovery, and how long it would take before the pain would subside. I think she was pretty used to this line of questioning from new patients; she handled it very professionally. She explained that she really couldn't tell me. The doctors would continue to assess my wounds every day until they decided what the best route would be for me. She told me the pain would get better, but she didn't know how quickly. I could feel she had empathy for me, and I knew she was telling me the truth. No matter how much I wanted to know when the pain would get better, no one would be able to tell me when that was going to happen.

The nurse went on to explain how my daily schedule would go: I would have some personal time until mid-morning. Then all of my bandages would be removed. The doctors would do a daily assessment of my wounds, after which an occupational therapist would come in to work with me on regaining movement. Once the therapist was done, the nurses would then give me a short sponge bath and re-bandage my body. For the initial stages of my stay, this was going to be my daily routine. In time, as my healing progressed, I would be allowed to leave the room and spend afternoons with an occupational therapist, doing additional exercises for strength, sensation and movement.

This conversation with the nurse lifted my spirits. It felt like there was something being done to assist my recovery – there was a plan beyond being drugged and left to lie in bed all day. These people knew what they were doing, and the difference between a burn unit and intensive care unit was obvious. The same hope that made me fight to survive on the island was coming back. I was alive in the care of a great hospital and I would get through this. That conversation with the nurse left me feeling the best that I had since the crash. I kept repeating to myself that I would get through this. I still didn't understand how difficult the time ahead of me would be.

Shortly after speaking with the nurse, I saw my parents through the large glass window. They entered the scrub room, gowned up, and came in to say good morning. I was feeling positive, and it was nice to have someone to talk to. I shared my enthusiasm and new excitement about my recovery with my parents and we had a good little visit.

I think my parents were relieved to see that I had renewed hope. It was still obvious how heavily my injuries weighed on them. Now that I am a father myself, I understand how difficult it must have been for my dad. Feeling helpless while watching your child in that kind of condition must have felt awful.

The nurses always gave me a needle of additional morphine before my morning activities. I like to think I am a tough guy with a high pain threshold, but I was thankful for the additional drugs when it came to the daily routine. After the injection came the unpleasant daily unwrapping of bandages. Sometimes I would get angry at the pain, but I apologized to the nurses for my anger the entire time. The nurses were fantastic; they did all they could to keep me calm and always tried all they could to avoid hurting me. They were my angels of the burn ward.

The doctors, by contrast, were always very matter-of-fact, almost cold, and lacked the empathy of the nurses. They were very straight to business, as I suppose a doctor should be. The early assessments were mostly about deciding whether or not I needed surgery to do skin grafts on my forehead.

The occupational therapist was a small East Indian man with a gentle demeanour, similar to the nurses. On his first visit, he explained that it was his job to get me functional again, and he took the time to explain how burn injuries affect the body's joints. It didn't take me long to figure out what he was really telling me: that he was going to grab my hands and force my fingers to move for me.

I could feel the anxiety and panic returning. Having my bandages taken off was painful enough, but this was different. I sure as hell wasn't ready to have someone grab my hands and start squeezing them shut for me. I started pleading with him to wait until tomorrow to get my fingers moving. I tried everything in my power to avoid what was about to happen. With a constant and gentle demeanour, he kept repeating that we had to get my fingers moving. He reached in and took hold of my left wrist with his right hand. He then went to place his left hand directly over mine. I started to involuntarily pull away.

He quickly tightened his grip on my wrist, and would not allow me to pull away. He placed his hand on top of mine, lining up his fingers individually with each of mine. The pain from his touch was brutal. He started squeezing his hand closed, forcing mine to do the same. The pain was excruciating; it seemed worse than being on fire. He only held my hand for about half a minute, and flexed my fingers about 15 degrees. Just enough to start to bend my fingers a little. When he let go, I pulled back and curled into a ball. He walked around the other side of my bed and did the exact same with my right hand. The experience on that hand was no better.

If given the option, I would have been sedated for this daily exercise. It is hard to explain, but everything seemed to happen in slow motion and at high speed at the same time. The seconds seemed long, but the experience seemed to end quickly. It felt like it actually twisted my mind somehow. I now knew that I would be doing the same agonizing exercise every morning. The anxiety this generated every morning was absolutely terrifying.

I knew the man was only doing his job. He didn't mean me any harm, and didn't want to see me in pain. After he was done, he quietly left the room. I often hated the world and was an angry person after these visits until I could talk myself into being positive again.

The nurses came back in to clean my wounds with a warm solution and re-bandage me. I grew to enjoy this time with my nurses. They were always gentle and didn't hurt me very much at all. It gave us time to talk as well. We never really got into anything too deep, mostly small chat, but it was one of my favourite times. This was the only real time I had to talk to anyone other than my family. I loved the fact that my family was around me all the time, but having other people to talk with was important.

I wasn't ready to talk about the crash yet, and I wasn't sure when I would be. I didn't want any visitors outside of my immediate family and three close friends from work. The afternoons seemed long, but I would always look forward to my family coming back in the evening. There was a lot of time to think and be alone, which was okay; I had a lot of stuff to work out in my head and my heart. The anxiety, the questions and the guilt of surviving were things that I battled with constantly.

On the second night in the burn ward, late in the evening after visiting hours had ended, the night-shift nurse came into the room and told me that there was a priest in the hallway asking if he could come and see me. The anger that I had felt toward God in my time of despair on the island had not yet diminished. I was confused about the brutality that had been inflicted upon me and wondered about God's role in it. I am not a particularly religious man, but agreed to speak with the priest to see where the conversation might go. It was a strange feeling, waiting for him to gown up and come into my room – anxiousness mixed with a calmness that I can't really explain.

The priest came into the room and over to the side of my bed. Although I am sure that he introduced himself, I can't remember his name. I wish I could remember his name. I would like to thank him for the difference he made that night, and in my recovery as a whole. Even now, in times of need, I find my thoughts going back to his words that night.

After introducing himself, he explained that he liked to come down to the burn ward in hope of providing comfort to patients, and to just be a good listener if they wanted to talk. He asked my name, and how I came to be in the burn ward. When I told him who I was, and talked about the plane crash, he smiled at me and said, "Oh, you are that very special man who survived."

Again, it is hard to explain, but from the way that he spoke and looked at me, I felt an immediate and deep warmness in my heart. The first thing he did was pay respect to the others by saying a prayer for them. He somehow knew that it was important for me to honour them. I spoke about my anger toward God for taking their lives, and the priest told me that he too thought this was a tragic loss of life that didn't seem fair or reasonable to us, but that we are not always meant to understand God's plan. He said that we could only mourn their loss and pray for them. He went on to say that we had to remember to pray for ourselves too. We had to pray for healing and peace even though we may never understand or accept tragic events. It wasn't his words so much that helped me start to find peace, but rather the way that he delivered them.

The priest turned his focus back to my survival. He had read some of the interviews from the rescue personnel about my unlikely survival and felt that it was a miracle that I was alive. He also believed there was a reason that I was still alive. In his words, "God had a purpose for me in life and, whatever that purpose was, I had not fulfilled it yet." I could feel how passionately he believed what he was saying, and it brought peace to my heart to hear someone else confirm my thinking, although at this point I hadn't associated God with my search for meaning. Who knows, maybe telling you my story and affecting one of your future decisions is that purpose?

The conversation with the priest was a powerful moment of impact in my life. After delivering his uplifting message, he quietly told me to get some rest and assured me that he would come back to see me again sometime. As quickly as he had appeared, he was gone. The priest never did come back, but I will always remember that conversation and the impact it had. Of all the special moments that helped me through my recovery to good physical, mental and spiritual health, this is the moment that affected me the most. I was still angry that the others had died, but now I believed there was a reason that I lived. It gave me something to believe in, and helped me deal with the guilt of surviving men that I considered better than me.

Day Three

At the time of the crash, I had been separated from my long-time girlfriend, Lasha. We had been together for six years previously, but were taking a break from our relationship. Lasha lived in Calgary, a three-hour drive south of Edmonton.

On the evening of day three, I saw her standing at the large glass window looking into my room.

Our reunion that evening was very emotional. On the Tuesday following the crash, Lasha had been reading the newspaper as part of her morning ritual and noticed an article titled "Edmonton Man, Sole Survivor of Plane Crash". She wondered if I knew the person, and started reading the article. When she saw my name in print and realized I was that survivor, she instantly felt sick to her stomach. She cried uncontrollably, with tears streaming down her face, as she told me about how she had found out what happened.

Lasha had contacted the hospital in Vancouver, but due to the security measures that had been in place to protect me from the media, the hospital would not confirm that I was there. My family had all left Edmonton to join me in BC, so she had been unable to contact them either. It wasn't until my family returned to Edmonton that Lasha was finally able to make contact and find out where I was.

Lasha refused to leave my side the night that she joined me in the burn ward at the U of A hospital. She broke the visiting hours rule and slept by my bed in an uncomfortable chair with her hand on my leg the entire night, just to let me know that she was there. My reasons for being distant from Lasha before the crash were all meaningless now, as they were with every other person in my life. As I watched her sleep, I reflected on how I had taken her for granted. I thought to myself, *if I would have died on that island, the last words that I would have said to her were not ones that I would have chosen her to remember me by.* It was another moment of impact that helped bring the mistakes of my previous ways into clear focus.

Day Four

On day four of the burn ward, I was told that I had been assigned a psychiatrist to help me through any potential post-traumatic stress disorder (PTSD). During our first meeting, I spoke about my commitment to become a better person, and how I was using this commitment to help give me strength to fight through the painful recovery. The psychiatrist told me that my strength and attitude were uncommon, and to keep doing what I was doing. My ability to generate positive self-talk had helped me through other difficult times in my life. Much like my conversation with the priest, the words of encouragement from this doctor were another confirmation that I was on a good path, and made me feel much better on the inside. I needed all the encouragement I could get, and coming from a psychiatrist made it that much more valuable.

Day Five

During my daily burn assessment on day five, the doctors concluded that I would not need surgery. I had to continue my daily routine while skin grew back over the burns, but I would not need skin grafts. Every morning, I would wake up in hope of the pain subsiding, even just a little; the re-growth of skin was the only thing that was going to reduce the constant and brutal pain.

Days 6 to 11

In the days ahead I would continue to process my feelings and slowly share the inner emotional turmoil with family and friends. Through these conversations we all grew closer and our relationships strengthened, which helped us in the healing process. I say helped "us" heal because it was hard for them too; it was hard for them to deal with my mood swings as I vocalized anger and grief. Hard to see me burnt, disfigured and in such pain. We were all on a healing journey together.

During this period, I was not allowed to see myself in a mirror; when we look outward through our eyes, everything looks the same to us. For my family and friends to look at me must have been tough; what they could see of my face through the bandages was burnt and swollen. I did not look like the same person, but they looked past that and saw me for the person they knew – not the disfigured person that I was at the time.

My sister Isobel and I have always been close. We share a bit of a twisted sense of humour so there were some much-needed laughs in the burn ward. My brother and I bonded again for the first time in a very long time.

My mother was the strongest of us all, as she has always been. She was there to hold me during the low times on my emotional roller coaster, when I would just break down and sob like a baby.

My dad's eyes were deep with pain for me. From his eyes, I could see that he would have taken my spot and my pain, if he could have. My father was there for everything and anything I needed or wanted. He is a strong man in every way. He kept me in line, and was there to listen anytime I wanted to talk. I came to realize how much I had taken both him, and his love for me, for granted.

Lasha played a major role in my recovery. I would talk most openly with her about how I was feeling and what I was thinking. She was a great listener, and helped me through a lot of difficult times that were to come.

The first lesson in my quest to become a better person was the realization that I had been taking my life, and the love of others, for granted. I needed to change that, and begin to appreciate the love that people had for me. Life is a precious gift, and our time on this earth is finite. I was humbled by the outpouring of love and support that I received from family and friends. Without them, I am not sure how I would have survived my time in the burn ward, and not lost my mind.

Day 12

I woke up every morning in anticipation of the pain diminishing. On the morning of day 12, when I opened my eyes, I could feel the pain had subsided, just a little. I was ecstatic to finally feel a little better, and very excited to share the news with my family. I was healing! I was filled with anticipation of getting out of this glass room and getting my independence back.

Day 12 was also the first day that my face would not be re-bandaged during the daily routine. I was thrilled not to have my entire head covered in thick, wet bandages. That morning, after the nurses removed the bandages from my head, one of the nurses that I had become very fond of asked if I would like to see myself in the mirror. I hadn't seen my own face in almost two weeks, and I was definitely curious as to what I looked like. I was afraid to look, but curious as well. The face that I saw looking back at me in the mirror was mine, there was no question of that, but I was not prepared for the way that I looked. I broke down crying. My face was covered in thick black scabs. I was ugly.

The nurse began to comfort me and said how good I looked. She told me I was fortunate that she could recognize all of my features, and that my face looked the same as the pictures in the newspaper. She assured me that I would look fine again once the scabbing was gone. I knew that I was fortunate, and that there are many other burn victims much worse off than I was. It took a few minutes, but eventually I managed to pull myself together and get over the initial shock. I took a longer look at myself in the mirror, and the nurse was right. I did still look like me, and that was something not all burn victims are blessed with.

My hands still needed daily bandages, but now each finger would be wrapped individually, allowing me to start touching things. I was now ready to begin pressure therapy on my face and hands. Pressure therapy works by forcing blood away from the surface of the skin. For example, if you take one finger and press firmly on the back of one of your hands for a few seconds and then remove it, you will see a temporary white area where your finger was. You have forced the blood away from the surface of your skin in this area. Keeping the blood away from the skin is imperative to preventing scarring and the only way to do that is to apply constant physical pressure. I learned that I would be fitted for a special pressure mask and pressure gloves for the following months to help minimize scarring.

The occupational therapists took a mold of my face and made a clear, hard-plastic mask that would fit over my face perfectly – similar to a goalie mask in hockey, but formed to fit every curve of my face. Straps were then mounted to the mask to hold it tightly in place. I was happy to be getting fitted for this mask as it meant that I was a step closer to getting out of the hospital.

Pressure gloves were also fitted perfectly to my hands. The gloves were made out of an elastic-like material that would keep constant pressure on all areas of my hands. Because the gloves were made out of material, there were a number of colours and designs to choose from. I went with plain black gloves in an attempt to be discreet and avoid drawing attention to them.

Day 12 marked the day that I was allowed to leave my room to start working full-time with the therapists on skin sensitivity, movement and strength rebuilding.

The brand-new skin covering my hands and fingers was ultra-sensitive. Cold seemed colder, hot definitely seemed hotter, and touching things like sharp corners with any amount of pressure would cause pain. We began work to desensitize my hands to the feel of things.

Early tasks for sensitivity were very simple. For example, the therapists would ask me to put my fingers into a bowl of marbles, move them around, and try to grab a handful of them. It sounded easy enough, but even that was difficult initially. I was shocked at how extreme everything felt. My mind would interpret how something should feel, but the nerves in my new skin were sending a much different message. The marbles were cold, hard and difficult to hold onto. Eventually I graduated from marbles to frozen peas, and then to uncooked rice in a bowl. The rice was the hardest: it felt like a thousand needles jabbing me all over, but I worked hard at it.

Hot and cold items were the hardest to desensitize my burns to. It was winter and in Alberta, Canada, winter is cold. Sensitivity of touch didn't really affect my face, but hot and cold sure did. My face was burnt worse than my hands, so this made temperatures seem extreme. Even if I tried to grab a can of soda out of a refrigerator with my bare hands, it would physically hurt me to hold the cold can. I logically knew that the can was not so cold that it should be hurting me, but the message my brain was receiving was: *The can is extremely cold and you need to drop it*. Progress was slow, but like the rest of my recovery, I pushed myself very hard. One of my therapists commented that she usually had to kick people in the ass to get them to try harder, but with me, she had to fight with me to slow down and stop pushing myself.

The occupational therapists helped with motor skills and movement. The new skin on my hands and fingers did not have a lot of stretch or flexibility to it. I could feel how tight the skin on my hands was, even after the morning torture sessions that I had already been through. I now had a better appreciation of the fact that those painful sessions had indeed served a helpful purpose. I was given simple tasks like screwing a plastic nut onto a plastic bolt. Again, that was way more difficult than I thought it should have been. Every aspect of regaining the use of my hands needed to be worked on. With hard work, I eventually graduated to exercises where the therapists would measure my grip strength. They started to give me real tools to do real tasks, such as hammering in a nail, or using a screwdriver. Doing these tasks with special tools measured how strong I was.

I pushed myself hard throughout all the physical therapy, determined to get my full independence back. I still had some emotional healing to do, but physically I excelled.

Day 14

Two days after getting the pressure therapy mask and gloves, I got my wish to be released from the hospital. New skin growth had minimized the risk of infection, and the pain was getting more manageable by the day. The next phase of my recovery would be as a day patient, returning to the hospital every day for continued work with the therapists and for periodic assessments by the doctors.

I was still not even close to being well enough to live on my own yet, so I would move to my parents' house so they could care for me for a while. The anticipation of getting back to the routine of daily life, and being engaged in it, brought me excitement. Christmas was coming soon, and I was looking forward to getting out to do some shopping. I know it sounds crazy, but the little things that we take for granted were big, exciting things for me at this point. Day 14 felt like the best day of my life.

ANOTHER BEGINNING

When I got out of the hospital, I was anxious to start living my life again little by little. I was happy to be out of the hospital, but I wanted to do more. I was ready to see co-workers and a wider circle of friends again. I wanted to go out and do some Christmas shopping by myself. I was in a rush to get back to "normal life". I wanted to put this difficult chapter of my life behind me.

My progress was good, but things did not happen overnight. It would still be a couple of weeks more before I was able to hold the steering wheel of a car and drive. My parents were great, and helped me throughout this phase of my recovery.

I quickly came to resent the pressure therapy mask and gloves – especially the mask. They were important and served a purpose, but the mask in particular was uncomfortable and restrictive. My skin couldn't breathe through the rigid plastic, which caused me to sweat. Despite the fact that the mask had been moulded specifically to my face, the pressure was not applied evenly. Some spots would rub more than others and hurt. I became so frustrated with it that one day I took a large metal file to the mask and ground down the edges around my eyes to make it a bit more comfortable. I knew the therapists wouldn't be happy about what I had done to my mask, but I didn't care; it was less painful to wear, and the sharp edges no longer drove into the skin around my eyes.

The mask also brought some emotional challenges and unwanted attention. After all, it was a full face mask, even if it was clear. Everywhere I went people would do a double-take or just stare. Now I must admit, it is not the type of thing you see every day – a guy walking around in a clear, full face mask in public.

The mask started at my chin and was moulded all the way up over my entire face, my forehead and the top of my head. The clear plastic on the top reflected light like a beacon. It had the same effect as a shiny bald head, but the clear plastic was unnatural, making me stand out even more. The constant looks made me very uncomfortable and self-conscious.

I tried to find some kind of solution to make myself stand out less in public. The best I could come up with was an old-style Fedora hat, large enough to cover the top of my head and reduce the bright reflection. In retrospect, this was probably not the best solution. The hat did reduce the glare from the top of my head, and made the mask less noticeable, but now I was a guy wearing black gloves, a plastic mask on his face and a weird old hat.

One evening, when I was able to drive again, I borrowed my parents' car to go to a mall and do some shopping. I was getting used to the stares, and thought that I could handle it. When we look out from our own eyes it is sometimes hard to see ourselves as different. On my list of things to shop for was a bracelet to replace one that I had lost in the crash. I didn't really think about the effect of walking into a jewellery store wearing a mask and gloves! It got everyone's attention right away.

The staff quickly realized that I was not a robber or a threat, but they still avoided serving me. They brushed me off when I tried to approach them for assistance. My short time in that store was another moment of impact. I had never felt like such an outcast as I did that evening. I was in a crowded shopping mall, surrounded by people, and yet felt very isolated and alone. I left the store, headed straight for the car and broke down crying.

At this point in my life it is fair to say that I was still somewhat emotionally fragile, but I am not going to let myself off the hook that easily. There was something bigger to be learned from this. I don't think anyone intentionally tried to hurt me or make me feel bad. I accept that, even if I forgot from time to time that I did look very different from the average person. Maybe some people assumed that I was some kind of freak who chose to wear an odd mask, but I think that most people didn't understand why I was dressed the way that I was. Either way, every stare hurt – even for a grown man.

I was out of the hospital, but not done learning lessons. This part of my learning journey really helped me to understand how it feels to be "different" or discriminated against. I have an entirely new understanding of how people with physical abnormalities, kids who look awkward, or people who have different cultural norms, must feel at times. I learned to do a better job of treating others as the normal people they are on the inside and to do my best to look past physical differences.

There is an old saying that goes: *"Sticks and bones may break my bones but words will never hurt me."* I think it is time that we parked that old saying. Words, even stares, can be just as hurtful as physical pain.

The weeks ahead were full of hard work, continued physiotherapy, small achievements, reconnecting with friends, and loving everyone that would let me love them. It was hard to try and come through this as a better person, but I felt like that hard work was paying off. I gradually met with all my friends, co-workers, and relatives who wanted to see me. With each get-together there were tears of sorrow for the lives lost and tears for the simple joy and appreciation of life. It was amazing how grateful I was for everything and everyone in my life. The days were not emotionally easy, but I was getting through them one at a time.

Four months after the crash, I returned to work. As expected, it was a little awkward at first. We were all close at Kiewit; so many of my co-workers were more like friends. Only the closest of them made me comfortable enough to talk about the crash. Most of my co-workers were glad to see me, but didn't really know what to say. It was a difficult subject for most people, and was avoided. For the most part, I was okay with that; I didn't know what to say to them either.

I initially told Kiewit that I was no longer willing to travel as part of my job responsibilities. The company was very understanding, and restructured my responsibilities to avoid travel. A few months later, when a remote project failed an audit for financial reporting, I felt compelled to go help out. I volunteered to travel to the site, but only temporarily to do an assessment.

When the assessment was completed, I further volunteered to be assigned to the project full-time to assist the site team with making necessary corrections. I knew that someone else could have taken over, but it was time for me to get back to what I was good at. The emotional stress associated with travel was decreasing. Life was returning to normal, and soon I was back to a "ten days on, four days off" rotation, working in a remote camp in northern Alberta. While I was getting more comfortable with the idea of frequent travel, the one condition that I did not waver on was my unwillingness to fly. Each rotation I made a six-hour drive to and from the site in my car.

A few months after I took the position at the remote site, I had lunch with my parents on one of my days off. I was surprised at what they said to me that day. Over lunch, they told me that they were happy and relieved that the crash did not change who I was. They went on to tell me that they were afraid that the crash would make me afraid of life. Afraid to be who I was and do what I was good at. Afraid to travel, even if that is what I needed to do in order to advance my career. I had always been passionate about my career, and they didn't want to see me lose that. I thought they would be upset that I was back to full steam ahead and working remotely, but they weren't. They were relieved that I was still the man I was before the crash. Maybe even perhaps a little improved, due to a new appreciation for life and the true value of our time on this earth with each other.

The lunch conversation with my parents that day was a moment of impact for me. It felt like a cornerstone in my recovery. The conversation caused me to pause and reflect on the great number of lessons that the crash had brought that had made me a better person. I was doing my ongoing best to be conscious of those lessons and to continue learning from them but something still felt missing.

I conceded that I might never understand why I had survived, but I kept searching for something more. My lessons and growth were far from over. In the years ahead, a series of unanticipated events helped to set me on a new journey.

HOLLYWOOD COMES CALLING

Two years after the crash, life had returned somewhat to normal. I was still assigned to the same remote project in northern Alberta, and was once again fully focussed on my career. I was home for the Christmas holidays when the phone rang.

The person on the other end introduced himself as Philip, a producer for a film company in Los Angeles. He asked me if I was the Tom Wilson who had been the sole survivor of a plane crash in November of 2008. I was a little uncertain about the legitimacy of the call, and it seemed a little strange coming out of the blue years after the event. At this point I had never spoken to anyone in the media. Even though I was a little uneasy with this call, the passage of time had made me a little more comfortable speaking about what had happened, so I told him that I was the person he was looking for.

Philip went on to tell me that his company had struck a deal with the Discovery Channel to produce a series of television shows on unusual survival stories. He had read a number of the articles related to our crash and was interested in my unlikely survival. He also commented on the fact that he could not find any interviews with me and asked why that was. I told Philip about my dislike for media sensationalism and the manner in which my family had been treated when I was in the hospital. I also told him that my recovery had been a very personal time for me; when the media was interested in talking to me, I wasn't interested in talking to them.

As our conversation went on, I learned that the program was going to be called "Sole Survivor" and that the production company wanted to share my story in the first episode. Philip asked if I could tell him my story. I wasn't going to share details with a stranger, but gave him a very brief summary of what had happened. He started pushing for more details, but must have recognized that he had intruded too far on my privacy for our first conversation and turned the conversation back to the proposed TV show. He told me to give the idea some thought, talk it over with my family and let him know if I was interested. I politely took his number and promised I would get back to him.

The thought of having my survival story as the first episode on a program on the Discovery Channel was very intriguing and a little exciting. But as I gave it more thought, I quickly turned against the idea. I remembered the sensationalism of the media during the initial crash coverage and imagined this experience would be no different. Besides, I didn't know if I wanted to tell my story to the whole world. I started thinking about the families of the men that died, and how they would feel about the show. It all got confusing very quickly.

I decided to take this decision to my family and closest friends to ask for their thoughts and perspectives. I knew that talking about it with them would help me make a choice. I think that I wanted them to vote against it. To my surprise, that was not the case.

Both family and friends thought that doing the Discovery TV show was the right thing to do. My family thought it could be a way for me to share my story, and inspire others to persevere through difficult times. Jody Sveistrup, a close friend and mentor from Kiewit, was supportive, and thought it was a good way for me to share my story with all those who wanted to know what happened that day, but were not comfortable enough to ask me.

There were many people who had been affected by the crash, and I had only shared details with my family and closest of friends. After weighing all the pros and cons, I decided in favour of the program to share some of the details of that day with those who would want to know what had happened.

With the decision to proceed made, I called Philip back to let him know that I was on board with shooting the program. A few days later, I had a conference call with Philip, the episode director, and a number of writers from the production company. At the end of the call they wanted to schedule me for a trip to their California studio for on-camera interviews.

This all seemed to be happening very fast, and I had some reservations about being interviewed. I shared my concerns about media sensationalism, and that the story be accurate. I also insisted that all who died be honoured and respected in the program. They told me that they would shoot the program based on my story, but they would retain all rights to editing before release. I would have no say in the final product. The production company was asking me to put a lot of trust in them. They reassured me that they had a good reputation and that the program was for a reputable network. Philip also made it very clear that I would receive no compensation for this – no one would be able to say that they "bought me" to say anything a particular way. They too wanted the honest truth.

I was having second thoughts about proceeding, so I did some research on the production company before agreeing to go ahead. I was also going to have to get on a plane to fly to Los Angeles for a day of interviews, which was still a bit scary for me. My travel was booked shortly after, and the decision was final. I had no idea what to expect, but I was excited about going to California and seeing the inside of a real production company.

I have to admit that prior to going to California, I let my imagination go a little, which probably affected my expectations. I envisioned a nice flight and grand hotel. I imagined the big studio and comfortable set. The experience turned out to be nothing like I had imagined.

My flights and hotel were booked with economy in mind. I arrived at the studio, courtesy of the studio receptionist in her personal vehicle. The "studio" was in fact an office building in an average part of town.

At the office of the production company, everyone seemed very busy and the office itself appeared a little disorganized. I stood alone at the front desk just long enough to begin feeling unimportant. Eventually a man and woman came over to introduce themselves. They were pleasant enough, but they were obviously rushed. They explained that we needed to get the interviews started to avoid running out of time before my return flight home that afternoon.

I was led to another large, empty room with only a folding table in a corner. I was given a blue golf shirt and asked to change into it as it would be better with the cameras and lights. After changing my shirt, I was immediately led into the interview room – a relatively small and windowless storage room with thick, black curtains attached to the walls. There were a couple of chairs beside some very bright lights and a camera pointed at a single steel chair in the middle of the room. The setting was not comfortable or welcoming at all; again, not what I had expected.

The entire experience to this point was unimpressive. I started to think this was a low-rate production company. This uncertainty affected my attitude, and I could feel myself becoming short and uncooperative as the interview began. After failing at some initial tense questions and answers, the director suggested that I just tell my story in my own words.

When I started to tell my story, I was still a little frustrated and had my guard up. Talking without interruptions allowed me get more comfortable and into a natural flow. I talked non-stop for what seemed like a couple of hours.

After telling the entire story, the director called for a short lunch break before regrouping to attempt a question-and-answer period again. I found the morning re-telling emotional and exhausting. I was tired, and needed a break. After a quick sandwich, I headed out to the front of the building to be alone. I was still a little uncertain if I was doing the right thing.

Back in the interview room after lunch, the director said that he was going to ask questions more than once to get different shots of me answering that question. He also explained that if I answered questions more than once, I was likely to remember more details about what happened. His first question was, "Can you describe what it felt like to wake up on fire?" I was surprised that he went straight to such a difficult question, but I was in a good state of mind so I did my best to answer.

He continued to ask difficult questions like, "How did you feel when you realized that everyone else was dead?" He repeatedly asked me questions about different parts of the story, but kept going back to how it felt to be on fire. The afternoon shooting became unpleasant and frustrating very quickly. I had already shared everything in detail, and didn't want to keep going over these difficult memories. Having to answer the same difficult questions over and over again started to make me angry. A short while into the afternoon session, and on about the fifth time the director asked me to describe being on fire, I lost my temper. With an angry scowl on my face, I raised my voice and replied, "What the fuck is it exactly that you don't understand about how it feels to be on fire from the last ten times I have explained it to you!?"

I was visibly upset, and decided that the interview was over. Even though they tried to be gentle with me, I was snappy. I asked for my shirt back, changed on the spot, and walked out of the room. I needed to get outside for a break and be alone for a while.

None of this experience matched my expectations. It felt like I had just been interrogated rather than interviewed. I had a feeling that the director had pushed me hard with his questions to bait me, and try and prompt more emotion from me during the interview. My dislike for media sensationalism resurfaced; I was concerned that this show might turn out to be more "infotainment" than a factual retelling of what had happened. The director had succeeded in stirring up old emotions in me, and I thought it was a shitty thing to do. I had just openly shared my personal story all day with these strangers in front of a camera and blinding light, with no say or control over the final product. Would they be respectful to the lives, the memories, and the families of those who had perished? I gathered myself as best I could and headed back up to the reception desk.

As soon as I walked into the office, the director and his assistant came over to me right away. They shook my hand and genuinely thanked me. They said I told my story very well, and they would do a great job of re-enacting the entire thing. They seemed like different people than the ones I just left behind in the so-called interview room. They told me they would have psychological and air-crash experts interviewed as well, and that they would do a very accurate re-enactment of the crash based on what I told them. At this point I had to trust these people; there was nothing else I could do.

Shortly after that, we said some polite goodbyes and I was on my way back to the airport. The experience of shooting a TV show in Los Angeles was over, and it was nothing like I had anticipated. I had finally broken my silence with the media and started to regret the decision to do the show at all. I was disappointed with the entire experience. I felt used.

I tried to push the whole experience out of my mind, but it continued to bother me. I wanted the program to be accurate, tasteful and professional; if any of the families of the men who died in the crash watched the program, I wanted them to know that it was all over very fast, with no suffering. All I could do was wait, and hope that the director and production company kept their word.

A CHANGE IN PERSPECTIVE

One evening, a few months after my trip to Hollywood, I received a phone call from my brother Mike. He had taken the lead on following up with the production company to get us a copy of the show. The previous day, a DVD labelled "Sole Survivor" had arrived in his mail. Mike had already watched the DVD, and told me that I would be okay with the way that the production company had produced it, but cautioned me that it was graphic and it might be difficult for me to watch.

That evening, Lasha and I sat silently on the couch in front of the TV and tried to mentally prepare to see the show. After a few moments, Lasha asked if I was ready. Once I nodded, she pressed the play button. The professional-looking opening sequence gave me some relief. I was concerned about how well this show was going to be done based on my low budget and tense experience at the California studios. It turned out that the show was very professionally done.

Lasha and I sat on the couch in silence, staring at the TV. As soon as the show started talking about the other passengers on the plane, a wave of grief came over me and I burst into tears. Lasha and I cried together the entire time we watched the show for the first time. As soon as it was over, she looked at me and asked if I wanted to watch it again. I absolutely did want to watch it again. The show stirred up a lot of emotions, but in some way it brought relief, and it felt good to cry about that day again.

When we were done watching the show together a second time, I could see that Lasha was very upset. She told me that even though she had already heard the entire story from me, seeing the re-creation on TV made it more real.

She had imagined what it must have been like to wake up on fire, but now that she saw what it was like, it made her very upset. Her response surprised me, but I understood it. The show evoked a similar response from many of my family and friends who saw it.

In the end, doing the program turned out to be a good decision. At first I was unsure that I made the right decision, but the end product was a good way for me to tell people the story, and help give others closure to what happened that day.

As time went on, news of the show began to spread at work. Almost everyone at Kiewit knew about the crash and my survival, so I wasn't really surprised at the amount of interest people had in the show. Over the next two years, I would play the DVD for many people who were interested. Some knew me very well and some did not. Eventually, I could make it through the show without crying, but my emotions would still get to me at random times for random reasons.

Discovery Channel eventually aired the series, and my story was the first episode played in the United States. As most of Kiewit's staff are based in the US, a number of them saw it. More people began approaching me and talking about what I had been through. This helped me to become more comfortable sharing my story which, in turn, helped put me on another path of healing and enlightenment.

CONVERGING ON A NEW PATH

Two years after the television show aired, I made a career move and left Kiewit to join another construction company. Once again, I was assigned to a project in northern Alberta. I had not watched the video in a while, but my reputation as the sole survivor of a plane crash seemed to precede me, and the topic started to come up in conversation with my new co-workers.

Early in my tenure at the new job, I joined the rest of the site workforce for a mass safety meeting. Mass safety meetings were a mandatory monthly event at each of our construction sites.

There were about 250 hourly workers and another 30 staff in attendance at the meeting. The topic for this meeting was "interventions". In the construction industry, an intervention is defined as the act of someone speaking up to correct an unsafe behaviour or situation, with the intention of preventing an incident or injury. Peer-to-peer interventions are always encouraged, because most workers work in pairs or groups. Leaders or safety professionals are not always with the workers, so it is important that peers watch out for one another and intervene when they identify something unsafe.

The downside of peer-to-peer interventions is that they can also result in conflict between peers. Big, tough construction workers do not always like being told that they are doing something that is perceived as "wrong". Different trade groups also have pride in their professions so interventions that cross trade lines can be delicate. The INTENTION of peer-to-peer intervention programs is good, but their resulting EFFECT can be negative if workers are not trained to do them properly. To be successful, companies also need to encourage and celebrate workers who participate in interventions to help make work sites safer for all.

I was enjoying the presentation at the safety meeting, but found it a little dry. The fellow leading the meeting kept pumping out statistics in a monotone voice, trying to convince his audience of the value of doing interventions. I looked around the large room and saw that most people did not seem to be paying attention. A few employees appeared to be sleeping; the rest seemed to be disengaged and sat fidgeting in their chairs waiting for the meeting to end.

As I watched the presenter struggling to get his point across and change the behaviour of his audience, I reflected on the biggest missed opportunity of my life to intervene. I could clearly see our pilot, Peter, looking back into the passenger cabin before takeoff and saying to us, "We are going to have to do some low-level flying because of the weather conditions. If anyone has a problem with that, let me know now and I will let you off."

Right there, in that moment, the idea of putting together a personal and powerful presentation on interventions became my personal mission. I was going to get out and share my story with audiences and help others learn from my experience.

That moment was a defining one for me, and a significant moment of impact in my life. After four years of searching, I had finally found the meaning of my journey. The pain, the suffering, the horror, grief, anguish and survivor's guilt that I had gone through were a gift. I had a calling, and that was to use my experience. I had to use this gift, to help to make the world a safer place.

I was going to save someone's life.

So this is the journey that I am now on; I may never know who, where or why, but I am convinced that it is going to happen.

Someday, as a result of hearing what I went through and what I have learned, someone, somewhere, is going to intervene or stop, think and make a safer choice that will save their life.

BRAVERY VERSUS COURAGE

After the epiphany that it was my mission to use my story to help and make the world a safer place, I began to think about, and analyze, the factors that led to our crash. My "day job" as a business manager took place at construction work sites, where there is a great emphasis on personal safety. I began to observe, read and research safety and human behaviour. What follows are some of the things I have learned.

Since the crash, I have been plagued with survivor's guilt. The terrible feeling that I should not have survived since the others did not. It is a pure statistical anomaly that I lived – a billion-to-one chance of pure luck.

In my case the guilt has been made worse by the feeling that I could have spoken up when our pilot, Peter, offered us the chance to get off the plane. It was a moment of impact that had escaped me. I was feeling uneasy about taking off in the poor weather conditions. What if I had found the courage to speak up and asked to get off? Could I have convinced my friends Kyle and Ajay to join me? What if three or four of us had opted to get off the plane? Would Peter still have continued with the flight or, with fewer passengers, might he have delayed the trip until conditions improved?

The difficult and honest truth is that I didn't speak up. I know that I should have, but I didn't. I had to take responsibility for my own actions and accept my contribution to the crash before I could begin to understand why others didn't speak up either. To this day, if there is a single moment that haunts me, it is that moment where I could have, and should have, prevented this tragedy. It is a feeling of regret that I don't wish on anyone.

Our pilot, Peter, owns the fact that he chose to fly in poor weather conditions. The conditions were so questionable that he even took the extra step of highlighting the danger to us and offering us the chance to get off the plane. Let me be clear: I am not pointing the finger of blame at Peter. We all owned part of what happened.

All of us missed the moment of impact in Peter's offer, and none of us passengers found the courage to take him up on it. We all own that. Again, I am not pointing the finger of blame at my peers; in fact, I hold myself more accountable than any of them for failing to speak up.

Lesson Number One

When there is a safety incident, everyone affected by it owns a piece of it.

All of us on that plane owned some accountability for what happened, but the big question is, "How did we get there?" What was so damned important about getting to work that Sunday morning that we all put our lives at risk by bravely accepting to fly in poor weather conditions?

There is a small clue in two specific words that I have chosen to use in the paragraphs above. We failed to find the COURAGE to speak up, and instead we chose to BRAVELY continue the flight. Have you ever thought about these two words? Let me make a distinction between them here.

I have come to learn that Bravery and Courage are not the same thing at all. When I was given a chance to speak up, I was a brave man, but I would not describe my actions as courageous.

I consider bravery as something associated with physical acts. People who "bravely march off to war" or "bravely put their lives on the line" for some higher purpose. Military, police and fire personnel all come to mind. They must be brave to carry out some of the high-risk activities in the line of duty of their chosen careers. That is not to say that they blindly accept all risks. In all professions we need to be forever looking at ways to continuously mitigate any unnecessary risks.

Courage, on the other hand, I consider to be an internal function more so than a physical one; courage comes from the choices we make in our mind when something does not seem right to us. The "courage to speak up" or the "courage to lobby for justice" are examples of this. In the face of pressure or danger, we make the choice to either be brave and accept the risk or we find the courage to speak up and voice our concerns.

After years of reflection, when I look back at that moment of impact – the chance to get off the plane –I realize that I was waiting for someone else to be courageous. If only one person would have spoken up and said they did not feel safe, I would have raised my arm in agreement and followed. I believe that at least some of the others would have joined in as well if someone had the courage to break the silence and speak up. I now understand that taking the risk to get the job done is bravery. Being a leader and protecting yourself and others by being courageous is often a harder choice than bravery.

As you read this, I am sure that you can remember a time when you faced an uncomfortable situation and chose to bravely go along with it rather than courageously speaking up.

Lesson Number Two

If we are going to make the world a safer place we need to foster more courage and less bravery.

Notwithstanding this distinction that we were being brave instead of courageous, it still does not answer the question of "how we got there", willing to fly in such poor weather conditions. The answer to this question is in one simple word: pressure.

Every one of us on the aircraft felt some kind of pressure to continue on with the flight. I can recall three different sources of pressure from that day: I felt career pressure, team pressure on behalf of the crew we were relieving and peer pressure on the plane itself.

At the time of the crash, I was an up-and-coming accountant in a large company. My future was promising, and I was determined to keep it that way. We all knew that the flight was important for production at the site. I felt the career pressure of being the person who might get in the way of production and end up being the guy scorned at the next managers' meeting.

We all knew that there were seven people up at Toba Inlet waiting to go home. The rotation at the Toba Inlet project was 21 days on and 7 days off; the men standing on the dock at the other end were anxiously waiting to get home to their families. I didn't want my name to get back to them as the person who had delayed or cancelled their return flight, and I suspect my fellow travellers all felt the same way. I didn't want to rock the boat, so to speak. I didn't want anyone to think of me as a nuisance. I put team pressure on myself to keep from speaking up and saying that I was afraid.

Even more immediate than my concern about letting down the crew at the other end of the flight was the on-board pressure. I was an accountant on a flight with a crew of tough construction workers, which in itself was a bit intimidating. If none of the others were going to say anything, I wasn't going to speak up and look like a coward. I gave in to unspoken peer pressure.

Some of the other passengers on the plane were contractors. While I was a salaried employee, some of them only got paid when they worked, so a day of delay was a day of pay to them. I am sure that this put pressure on them to want to get to the work site.

Our pilot must have been dealing with various pressures of his own. Peter had a lot of experience, and was well known for his abilities as a bush pilot. Like many of us, I would guess that Peter was proud of his reputation. Unbeknownst to us, did Peter have a special dinner planned with his wife or an appointment with his doctor in the afternoon? Maybe he felt schedule pressure; there were two flights in and out of Toba Inlet each day, using the same aircraft, so maybe there was pressure to get both flights in. Peter would also have realized that the crew coming out was anxious to get home to families, and some may have had connecting flights that they had to catch.

There is also the possibility that he was feeling some of the same pressures that we were, the pressure to be the guy who would bravely get his job done.

Our Kiewit leaders wanted us to travel safely and I know that, in retrospect, they wished the flight had not taken off when it did. As for the crew waiting for the flight home, as it turns out, their flight was cancelled for the next three days during the crash investigation. Seven good men died as a result of pressure we all put on ourselves.

Lesson Number Three

Pressure can lead to people bravely putting themselves at risk rather than being courageous enough to speak up.

Pressure exists; we can't just wish it away. Ironically, pressure and a certain level of stress have been proven to be good things to help keep us attentive and productive. However, not all pressures are created equal. Any and all pressure related to safety must be held sacrosanct. As leaders, we must be aware of the danger that results when we apply pressure on others to take risks. Furthermore, we must also be cognizant of the perceived pressure that we put on others by the kinds of things that we reinforce. If we celebrate the "firefighters" or "git-er-done" heroics of employees who take risks to achieve good results, we are reinforcing a silent pressure that results in risk-taking.

RETURN TO THE ISLAND

In 2014, I decided to return to the island for the first time since the crash. As soon as I started to organize the trip, it quickly became apparent that fate would be involved one more time.

I made a call to Station 12 of the Royal Canadian Marine Search and Rescue office in Sechelt to let them know about the trip, and to see if they would be interested in meeting my family while we were in the area. My call was quickly returned by Bob McKee – the man who had pulled me into the Zodiac and had taken care of me on the boat ride across the bay to the waiting ambulance.

Bob arranged everything. He managed to get the original coast guard rescue team together to take us back to the island. He even arranged for the trip to take place in the same red Zodiac rescue boat. Bob also got in touch with the ground search and rescue team who had located the plane after I was picked up. The ground team insisted on mapping everything out and accompanying us both to and from the crash site. Every single person volunteered their entire day to be with us and take us back to the crash site. Their wonderful response to our little reunion was overwhelming.

We were greeted warmly on the morning of our arrival at the coast guard dock. It brought me deep pleasure to personally thank, hug and talk to every one of the rescuers who were involved in my survival that day. They genuinely appreciated the fact that I came back to say "thank you". As we talked, they each had a story to tell about the day, and a different perspective on how it had impacted them. Their stories reminded me yet again of how many lives were affected that day.

One anecdote that I had previously been unaware of was that there were two local hunters on the island that day: Al "Bunny" Hailey and Fred Severre. Fred heard what he thought was a plane crashing into the trees on the foggy mountain, and alerted the local authorities on his cell phone. Given that the emergency transponder on board the plane was destroyed in the crash, without Fred's phone call it might have been much later before help arrived.

And so it was that in November of 2014, on the sixth anniversary of the crash, I returned to Thormanby Island for the first time. Lasha and my friend Stephen joined me, and with the help of the original rescue team we hiked up the mountain to erect a cross in honour of the men who had died.

We climbed through the trees and approached the crash site from the opposite side of the island. The ground rescue team had decided that it would be best to hike in via an old logging road and to hike out along the path I had originally taken back to my point of rescue.

When we found the crash site, there were two other crosses that had been erected by the families of Matt Sawchenko and Jerry Burns. We erected our cross nearby, and I began to pray.

I asked God to welcome and comfort the men that he had called home on the day of the crash. I asked him to bring strength and courage to the mourning families; even though they may never find understanding, I asked that he somehow help them find peace. I thanked him for the strength and courage he gave me and my family, and I thanked him for the gift of life that I was given that day. I thanked him for the changes that he had brought to my life and for my beautiful family. I asked him for the courage to continue to live my life in a way that would not waste the precious gift I had been given. I had not been able to attend any of the funerals because I was hospitalized, and until this day I had never had an appropriate opportunity to pray for the seven. In that moment, I felt very spiritually connected to the crash itself and the deceased.

With the November daylight starting to fade, we paid our respects and started searching through the trees to find my original path down the mountain. This time I wasn't injured and I wasn't alone; I was healthy, and with people that loved and cared about me. Before long, we found the cliffs that I had slid down and the landing area just below it. We continued through the bush and found the creek. As we walked the creek, I talked about how pissed off I had been when the helicopter had flown over. I was in awe to be walking this same path again. Before long, we came out through the bush to the inlet.

As I stood at the shore at the apex of the inlet, and looked out over the ocean at the houses across the bay again, six years of time suddenly evaporated. I remembered standing at that exact spot, thinking that I would never see any of my loved ones again. I remembered being angry at God for burning me and taking my life away, as I lost all hope of being rescued. I also remembered Bob and his crew coming into the inlet, and how incredibly good that felt.

The return to the island brought me a great deal of spiritual closure that I hadn't realized was missing. I turned to Lasha, and held her as we stood there on the shore. Then I thanked God one more time for the precious gift he gave me that day.

Tom meeting rescuer Bob McKee again for the first time in six years.
Photo by Lasha Paramchuk

Tom and the rescue team who helped him to return to the island on the sixth
anniversary of the crash. Photo by Lasha Paramchuk

Left to right: Peter Forster, George Lyske, Bob McKee, Alan Skelley, Tom Wilson,
Alec Tebbutt, Richard Till. Original rescuers missing from the photo: Ron
Dinsdale and Drew McKee.

Tom and Lasha with the cross dedicated to the Seven at the shore of Thormanby Island. Photo by Stephen Quesnelle

Tom and local hunter Al "Bunny" Hailey. Photo by Stephen Quesnelle

Hiking to the crash site. Left to right: Alec Tebbutt, Tom, Lasha, Al "Bunny" Hailey and Richard Till. Photo by Stephen Quesnelle

Tom and ground rescuer Richard Till discuss the path to the site. Photo by Stephen Quesnelle

Tom at the crash site examining a piece of the wreckage. Photo by Lasha Paramchuk

Ground rescuer Richard Till describes the crash debris trail to Tom and Lasha. Photo by Stephen Quesnelle

Ground rescuer Alec Tebbutt stands in the V-shaped path of destruction carved by the aircraft. Photo by Lasha Paramchuk

Tom visits the memorial cross of Matt Sawchenko at the crash site.
Photo by Stephen Quesnelle

Tom and the memorial cross to the Seven. A memorial cross for Jerry Burns is on
the right. Photo by Stephen Quesnelle

Descending the mountain again on Tom's original path.
Photo by Stephen Quesnelle

CLOSURE

I never imagined that I would be in a plane crash. I had no idea what life had in store for me when I woke up on the morning of November 16, 2008. How I wish I could take that day back and bring the others back to their families. I can't go back and seize my opportunity to speak up and change the day's outcome. I can't change anything about what happened that day.

If I could have avoided ending up in a burn ward, I would have. I still remember how long and agonizing every moment seemed. I still remember the anxiety of anticipation before various procedures. I would have given anything for the pain to end. The pain of the families that lost their sons, husbands, brothers and fathers in that crash was deep and unforgiving. Their pain was worse than mine, and I am sure that it continues to this day. If I could take that pain away, all of it, without hesitation, I would.

I have worked hard at becoming a better person, and I am thankful for what I have learned as a result. I have searched hard for meaning in the seemingly senseless deaths of my friends and co-workers, and the search has set me on a new path as a way to honour them.

I am still trying to get over my survivor's guilt. I have had to accept what happened and come to terms with it. Every time I speak publicly about safety, I feel like I am paying tribute to the others in a way that effects positive change and may even save another's life. This tribute has helped me heal. Doing public speaking and writing this book have both helped to bring me some closure.

My priorities have changed. Who I am and what is important to me all changed because of that terrible experience. Lasha and I went on to have two beautiful daughters, who breathe life and spirit into me. They are the sweetest thing that God has ever blessed me with.

When I was in the hospital burn ward and the priest came to see me, I needed answers and faith. He gave me the answers that I needed, which fuelled the faith that I was desperately searching for. That faith moulded my approach throughout the rest of my struggle to recovery. The priest told me that there was a reason I was alive, and that I was somehow special. Just like I needed hope of rescue on the island, I held onto the priest's words to help get through the difficult path ahead of me. My conversation with that priest was one of the most memorable and defining moments in my recovery; it did not take away my anger or confusion about what had happened, but it gave me the faith I needed to get through it.

One evening, as we discussed an early version of the manuscript for this book, my co-author and friend, Stephen, asked if I thought the priest was real or if I had imagined him. I wasn't surprised by the question, as I have often asked myself the same thing. I don't know if the priest was real flesh and blood, but someone, or something, visited me that night, and their message was very real. The crash, the priest, and the entire experience of all I went through changed my relationship with God.

In the past, I had only searched for God in my darkest hours. Only when I needed help would I turn to him. After my experience in the burn ward, I started to look for him in my life when it wasn't so dark out. I began to ask him for the strength and courage to get through what it was he chose to put in front of me. I began to understand that I am not in control of all the events that happen to me, and that I am only holding the road map in the bigger scheme of things. I have come to believe that there is a path in front of all of us, and that choices are presented along the journey; it is up to us to do our part and make the right choices. I believe that God gives us strength and courage when we need it the most, but I also believe it is up to each one of us to find meaning in our lives.

I feel like I am ready to move on now. I am proud of how I came through all that was put in front of me, and I am proud of who I became because of it. I have found a small way to bring good from a day filled with tragic loss. I have found a way to honour and remember the lives that were lost that day. Going back to the island to erect a cross in honour of the seven has helped me make my peace with God. I walked the path that I described earlier in this book, and was able to share the experience with Lasha and a good friend.

Going back to the island seemed to bring it full circle – to validate my journey somehow. The return gave me new memories of the island, which now brings me to a point where I feel like I have found closure, and am ready to move on to the next chapter in my life. A chapter full of appreciating and valuing every moment I have as a son, a father, a brother and a friend. I don't know what lies ahead of me, but I will do my best to learn from it, continue to grow and be a better man because of it.

BOOK 2

MAKING THE WORLD A SAFER PLACE

In the prologue at the beginning of this book, I promised to tell you my story in two parts. Book 1 is the story of the fateful airplane journey and the events that followed. As we begin Book 2, the nature of this book will shift. In the pages ahead, I will discuss the role of human behaviour in safety, and what we can all do to make the world a safer place.

To give some context to Book 2, let's begin with a few excerpts from the official investigation report (Transportation Safety Board of Canada Aviation Investigation Report A08P0353, authorized for release August 11, 2010), which shows that a combination of factors across various stakeholder groups contributed to the incident.

Crash Investigation Findings

The Transportation Safety Board of Canada Aviation Investigation Report on the crash revealed the following:
[Previous Accident].

"The weight and balance completed by the pilot indicated that the aircraft was within limits for the accident flight. However, incorrect passenger and fuel weights had been used and the pilot's weight not included...although the aircraft was within centre of gravity limitations, it was likely about 75 pounds over the maximum gross weight at takeoff." (Page 4)

"Pacific Coastal management had met with the pilot three times to discuss concerns they had with his decision-making. The last meeting, about

three months before the accident, was held because management was concerned that he was completing trips in what other pilots deemed to be adverse wind and sea conditions. The company believed this behaviour was causing other pilots to feel pressured to fly in those conditions and was also influencing customer expectations. At least one fishing lodge owner favoured the accident pilot because he flew customers in and out when other Pacific Coastal pilots would not because they felt the conditions were too risky." (Page 5)

"The day before the accident [another] pilot ...made a precautionary landing to wait out... [poor weather] conditions. That pilot subsequently observed a Pacific Coastal Grumman Goose fly by...records show that the Grumman Goose was piloted by the accident pilot." (Page 6)

"The Merry Island lighthouse is located along the intended route about 3 miles southeast of the accident flight. Weather observations are taken and reports issued every three hours. The lighthouse keeper who issued the weather reports on the morning of the accident did not have instruments...to accurately measure all the parameters contained in the report. Investigators found that the shoreline reference used to estimate the 600-foot [cloud] ceiling was actually at an elevation of about 300 feet." (Page 9)

[Previous Accident]. "On 03 August 2008, a Pacific Coastal Grumman Goose was in an accident...the aircraft had crashed into a mountainside and was destroyed. A post-crash fire occurred. Of the seven occupants, the pilot and four passengers were fatally injured." (Page 10)

"Following the 03 August 2008 accident, Pacific Coastal initiated a risk analysis of its VFR [Visual Flight Rules] operations. This risk analysis was not completed because of insufficient in-house skill in formal risk analysis methodologies." (Page 12)

"TC [Transport Canada] also found that it was unclear if the company [Pacific Coastal] had examined supervisory and organizational factors following the 03 August 2008 accident." (Page 14)

"While flying out of Vancouver, the two [Pacific Coastal] VFR pilots were informally monitored by the Vancouver management team whose offices were adjacent to the crewing room. However, no formal reporting method was established for these pilots and neither of them attended pilot meetings…" (Page 12)

[Perceived safe low-level flying] "Beliefs, combined with competitive pressures and the difficulty of enforcement, lead to situations where some pilots and operators are willing to take risks by flying in marginal weather conditions. Left unchecked, these practices become accepted norms and are adopted by new pilots." (Page 15)

"The aircraft's GPS was not recovered, so it is not possible to determine the settings at the time of the accident. However, given the altitude of the flight, if the GPS was functional and if the terrain-and-obstacles alert was in the active mode, it would have displayed a terrain-and-obstacles alert almost continuously." (Page 22)

"During his pre-flight briefing, the pilot advised the passengers that the flight would be conducted at low altitude and that, if they were concerned, they could deplane. This is not a normal part of the pre-flight briefing and indicates that the pilot was aware that the weather along the route was likely to be poor enough that, in order to maintain ground reference, the flight would have to be conducted at a lower altitude." (Page 23)

"The pilot's commitment to the decision to depart would have increased after boarding passengers, loading luggage, and starting the engines." (Page 24)

"The pilot did not request the latest available weather reports…" (Page 24)

Risk Tolerance

While all of us on the plane that day felt some kind of pressure to continue with the flight in poor weather conditions, we can now ask, "Why did we accept the risk?"

Risk Tolerance should not be confused with the ability to identify a risk. There is a level of skill and experience that helps us to identify all of the things in our environment that pose a risk. Risk Tolerance, however, is simply our willingness to accept or reject risk in the moment that we are presented with it. When faced with a risk, if our tolerance for that risk is HIGH, we are more likely to perform the task. If our tolerance for the risk is LOW, we are likely to reject the task.

I believe there are 10 factors that contribute to our personal level of risk tolerance. Every person is different, and every one of us has a different tipping point, which divides our acceptance or rejection of risk based on a combined weighting of the factors. The ten factors are:

1) Capability and Experience
2) Familiarity with Task
3) Seriousness of Outcome versus Likelihood
4) Voluntary Actions/Perception of Control
5) Personal Experience with an Outcome
6) Cost of Non-Compliance
7) Confidence in Equipment
8) Confidence in Protection and Rescue
9) Potential Profit or Gain from Actions
10) Role Models and Peers Accepting Risk

In the following explanation of each of these ten factors that contribute to Risk Tolerance, I am going to share my perspective on how they relate to the crash from the perspective of the pilot. I did not know our pilot, Peter, personally, but I do know that he did not want to die and I lay no blame. I am using this example here as an illustration only.

1. Risk Tolerance Factor – Capability and Experience

The first factor relates to our level of capability and experience with the task at hand. If we have a high level of skill with the task, or very similar tasks, and have experienced success (positive outcomes) in the past, we are more likely to accept the risk of the task.

Our pilot was a very experienced bush pilot with excellent capabilities. He had many hours of flying experience, and had managed to fly successfully in poor weather conditions in the past. Peter's skill as a pilot and confidence in his capabilities may have contributed to his tolerance for risk and his choice to fly on that foggy November morning.

Experience and strong capabilities can feed the belief that, "It won't happen to me – it hasn't yet, and I have been doing this for a long time." We begin to believe that our level of skill will arm us against negative consequences for taking risks. Experience is a valuable asset, but can also lead to overconfidence, and increase tolerance for risk.

2. Risk Tolerance Factor – Familiarity with Task

Familiarity with Task, although similar to Capability and Experience, has more to do with a specific task and the number of times we have performed that same task. If we apply this factor to the plane crash, it would relate more to the specific route that Peter was planning to take than his overall experience as a pilot. The more often a specific task is repeated successfully, the higher the tolerance for task risk becomes over time.

Peter was very familiar with the route planned on that morning. He typically flew the same route every day, often more than once per day. The familiarity and comfort of the same flight path may have influenced Peter's willingness to accept the risk of flying in foggy conditions.

3. Risk Tolerance Factor – Seriousness of Outcome versus Likelihood

The Seriousness of Outcome answers the question, "What is the worst that could happen?" while the Likelihood of Outcome answers the question, "How often does it happen?" The more serious the potential consequence, the less likely we are to accept risk, especially when paired with a high likelihood. For example, many people would put an activity like skydiving in this category; it has a highly serious outcome, and a fairly high likelihood of something going wrong. By contrast, driving a car down a two-lane, non-divided highway has a high potential seriousness of outcome, but an experienced driver will consider the likelihood of negative outcome as low.

Similarly, I believe that every person on the plane understood how serious the outcome of a plane crash would be. The awkward silence that followed Peter's offer for us to get off indicates that we were all thinking about the likelihood of the outcome on that particular day. The tipping point for me, and maybe for the others, was Peter's assurance that if things got bad we would be back at the airport having coffee in 20 minutes. In my mind, this statement diminished the likelihood factor, and led me to give the "thumbs-up" vote of proceeding with takeoff. With a high seriousness but lower likelihood of negative consequence, I was willing to accept the risk.

4. Risk Tolerance Factor – Voluntary Actions/Perception of Control

The ability to choose a task voluntarily influences the willingness of a performer to accept the risk associated with it. A performer who carries out a task "because it was their idea" may be willing to take more risk.

In selecting a task, the performer evaluates all available consequences (either consciously or subconsciously) and opts for the course of action that they perceive as either the most net positive or least net negative in nature, even if the positive consequences are only generated internally (for example, in the form of self-talk).

In our situation, I think it was within Peter's control to decide whether or not to fly. He seemed enthusiastic and ready to go. He also involved us in the decision, and asked for our input on the decision to take off, giving us a level of control that we failed to use wisely.

Once a performer decides to perform a task and takes steps toward it, they tend to look for data that supports their decision, and avoid or reject data that does not support their decision.

With the decision to fly made, and the luggage and passengers on board, Peter's commitment to his decision to take off would have strengthened. There is evidence to suggest that he did not utilize the full capability of the onboard GPS and did not request the most recent weather reports.

5. Risk Tolerance Factor – Personal Experience with an Outcome

Previous outcomes experienced following a task have a direct correlation with the likelihood of the task being repeated again. A task that is followed by a positive consequence is more likely to be repeated than a task that is followed by a negative consequence. If a task involves a certain level of risk, and if the completion of the task is frequently accompanied by a positive consequence, the performer is MORE likely to accept the risk and repeat the task. This results in an increased risk tolerance.

In our case, none of us had ever experienced a plane crash before. We all had experienced some minor bad consequences like turbulence or delayed flights, but in all cases the overwhelming positive consequence was that we had arrived at our destination safely. This past consequence history raised our level of risk tolerance, and was a contributing factor to our agreement to fly. Peter had received positive feedback from past customers for flying in difficult weather conditions. He was their "go-to" guy.

6. Risk Tolerance Factor – Cost of Non-Compliance

The Cost of Non-Compliance refers to the magnitude of the penalty for accepting a risk. For example, we all know that driving a car at high speed increases the probability of getting a fine, yet many people speed at times because the combination of the chance of getting caught along with the size of the fine is too low to deter the act. Many people speed because the cost of non-compliance (the cost to them of speeding) is low, which raises their risk tolerance for the act. If the consequence, or cost of noncompliance, is low, a person is more willing to accept the risk of getting caught performing a task that is out of compliance with safety.

The Transport Canada investigation into the crash identified that some basic flight regulations had not been followed. While there may have been a monetary cost to non-compliance in the form of fines, this "cost" was not perceived as high enough by those involved to have kept the flight from departing.

7. Risk Tolerance Factor – Confidence in Equipment

Confidence in Equipment will also influence the willingness to accept risk. Imagine how you would react if someone asked you to climb up on to the roof of a very high building using a dilapidated old ladder. If your confidence was low that the ladder would hold you, it is likely that you would refuse the task.

The plane we were on that morning was about 50 years old. Peter was very familiar with the aircraft; over the years he had developed almost a respect for, and a working relationship with, the plane. Due to maintenance requirements, the plane was in good mechanical condition, but it lacked modern avionics and instrumentation, which may have helped to avoid the crash.

8. Risk Tolerance Factor – Confidence in Protection and Rescue

Confidence in the quality and availability of protection and rescue influences our decision-making in the presence of risk. This type of behaviour is often seen in the underground mining industry. A great deal of safety precautions are put in place to be able to protect and rescue miners in the event of a mine collapse.

I will admit that rescue was the last thing on my mind before we took off on our flight, and was not a factor in my decision to stay on board the plane. When I was standing badly burned, half-naked and shivering from the wind on the shore of Thormanby Island, I was hoping and praying for a rescue team to find me before I died of exposure.

9. Risk Tolerance Factor – Potential Profit or Gain from Actions

The presence of strong positive consequences can influence people to raise their risk tolerance. This is particularly dangerous when leaders in a position of power trade off the safety of large numbers of workers in exchange for their own personal gain.

I am not sure how Peter was compensated, but many airlines do not begin to pay their employees until the cabin door is closed. Time on the ground with the door open is not paid for, so he might have felt payday pressure, which might have been one of the factors in his decision to depart.

10. Risk Tolerance Factor – Role Models and Peers Accepting Risk

We are all influenced by the actions of our role models and peers; watching people that we trust and respect accept certain risks can motivate us to do the same things. Conversely, if we see our role models rejecting risk when faced with it we are more likely to follow suit as well. We are all role models to some degree either at work, in our homes, or in social groups; we need to be self-aware of this and be respectful of the way that we influence others.

I will admit that I felt unspoken peer pressure from my friends and co-workers, which influenced my decision to continue on with the flight despite my concerns about the weather conditions.

I hope that these 10 risk tolerance factors can be of some value to you. If you are in a position of either assessing potential risks or analyzing an incident, it is important to note that all 10 are not necessarily present in every situation. On the other hand, I am sure that you will find at least one or more of them to be present in most situations.

I am going to turn the next chapter over to my friend and behavioural expert Stephen Quesnelle to share his thoughts on behaviour-based safety.

BEHAVIOUR-BASED SAFETY

Let me begin by dispelling a myth; some people are under the impression that behaviour-based safety is a program for blaming frontline workers who get injured. In fact, nothing could be further from the truth.

Firstly, behaviour-based safety is not a program. Programs come and go like fads. Behaviour-based safety is a methodology rooted in Applied Behavioural Science.

Secondly, a behaviour-based safety approach focuses on understanding, analyzing and improving the factors that influence safe behaviours at ALL levels in the organization. Often the root cause of a poor safety culture lies not with the frontline employees, but with the behaviour of managers.

I am going to cover four topics in this chapter. We are going to define behaviour, look at the factors that prompt behaviour to happen, consider the consequences that sustain behaviour, and lastly we are going to take a look at the two different kinds of incidents.

Behaviour

Behaviour is one of those often-used words that can have a wide range of definitions and interpretations. I prefer a very simple definition: Behaviour is an action that requires muscle movement. Words like "motivated", "lazy", "loyal", "dangerous", "dedicated" and "sloppy" are what we call labels. Labels are generalizations and not behaviours. It is nearly impossible to communicate to someone that we need more of a good behaviour or less of a poor behaviour unless we can communicate what "it" is in precise terms. Labels permeate our day-to-day speech, and learning to communicate expectations in behaviourally pinpointed terms is very difficult for some. The ability to communicate safe behaviours in a behaviourally pinpointed manner forms the foundation of a good safety system. Consider these two examples:

"Hey, Jimmy, grab somebody and get these posts loaded into the truck pronto! We've gotta get on to the next job." Or:

"Jimmy, go get Don to help you load these posts into the back of the truck. Be sure to talk to one another before lifting each one to ensure that you are both ready. Remember to use your legs and not your backs when lifting. I want you both to get your gloves on and pick the poles up on the side to keep your hands out of any pinch points. As soon as you are done, come and get me so that we can move to the next job. What questions do you have of me before you begin?"

As you can see, the first example leaves a lot of things open to interpretation, and has some implied pressure to move quickly rather than safely. While this might look simple and obvious, teaching supervisors and managers to speak in behaviourally specific terms is one of the greatest challenges that I face as I teach them about behaviour-based safety. Setting expectations in behaviourally specific terms sounds easy enough, but for many it requires a great deal of practice to master.

Factors That Prompt Behaviour

Behavioural prompts or activators are known as "antecedents" or, as I prefer to call them, "the factors that set people up to perform tasks safely". There are four particular behavioural enablers that are critical to a safe work environment: what, how, with what and why. Before someone can perform a task safely, they need to know WHAT it is that is expected of them (the pinpointed behaviour discussed above), HOW to do it, WHAT TO DO IT WITH and WHY it is necessary to be done a particular way.

HOW to do something often comes from some form of training; the more complex the task, the more extensive the training needs to be. However, there is more to successful safe behaviour than just training. When a safety incident occurs, training is often falsely singled out as the root cause.

To do a task safely and successfully, people need the TOOLS AND RESOURCES with which to do it. Many organizations provide their employees with Personal Protective Equipment (PPE) such as earplugs, safety glasses and gloves to ensure that they have the resources to work safely. However, items such as machine guards, proper ladders and lifting equipment might also be required for some tasks to be completed safely.

The fourth antecedent category is the understanding of WHY something needs to be done a particular way. This is often the quickest and easiest of antecedents to provide to workers, and it is the most often forgotten element of setting others up for safety success.

The Consequences That Sustain Behaviour

Antecedents are the factors that set people up to be able to work safely, but even the best antecedents are useless unless paired with appropriate and timely consequences. The 10 risk tolerance factors that Tom presented in the last chapter are mostly a function of consequences. After a person has done a behaviour once, they will quickly decide whether or not to do it again based on what happens to them.

Here are a couple of important things about consequences to note: After every behaviour, we receive MULTIPLE consequences. Some we give ourselves in the form of self-talk, like the feeling of pride we take in a job well done or the feeling of embarrassment for letting others down; some consequences we get from mother nature (things like the taste of food, electrical shock or sunburn) and some consequences come from others, like peers who tease us, the boss who praises us or the salesperson who smiles at us in the check-out lane at the grocery store.

In addition to the multiple sources of consequences, all consequences are not equally powerful; there are four different dimensions to consequences that alter their strength.

Timeliness: Some consequences are more powerful because they immediately accompany the behaviour. Consider how it feels to eat your favourite food. The biological system of your taste buds gives you a timely positive consequence when you eat something you really like. Similarly, think about putting your hand on a hot stove. Again, Mother Nature provides you with a timely negative consequence that changes your behaviour quickly as your pull your hand away! The more timely the consequence, the more influence it will have on our behaviour.

Like/Dislike: We like some consequences and we dislike others. In general, we find some consequences to be positive and others negative. For example, people enjoy getting a raise at work (a positive consequence) and dislike getting a speeding ticket (negative consequence). In general, we seek out positive consequences that we like and avoid negative consequences that we dislike.

Importance: We all care about some consequences more than others, and we tend to value consequences with larger magnitudes. Tom's discussion about the "Cost of Non-Compliance" highlights this element of consequences. Certainly the risk of getting a speeding ticket does not compare to the risk of losing your life in a plane crash. Bigger risks are more important to us, and influence our behaviour more strongly.

Certainty: As I mentioned earlier, after every behaviour we receive multiple consequences. However, the certainty of these consequences materializing may, or may not, be consistent. You can say with certainty that every time that you put your finger into a live electrical socket, you will receive a shock, but every time that you do a good job at work, there is no guarantee that the boss will notice it or praise you.

It is this element of "source" that enables good leaders to create a culture of safety. Effective leaders create an endless supply of free, timely and positive consequences for employees who do the right/safe things. By doing so, these leaders offset the other consequences that may be urging the performer to take an unsafe shortcut or some other kind of risk. Of course, remembering to do this consistently completes the "certainty" portion of the consequence equation.

In the paragraph above, I refer to the timely, positive consequences as free because they take the form of feedback. Providing timely, positive feedback for safe acts is one of the few examples of where "reminding" someone of something actually helps to produce effective behaviour-shaping.

In the case of the Thormanby airplane crash, we can use the critical behaviours of "closing the cabin door" and "all giving the thumbs-up to agree to take off" as a good point to perform a consequence analysis for both the pilot and passengers. The majority of the consequences for the pilot and passengers were all Timely, Positive, and Important to them and Certain; once in the air they were all getting closer to their destination second by second. There was the possibility of crashing into a mountainous island, but that was NOT Timely (it took 20 minutes of flight time). The possibility of a crash was also Negative and Important but NOT Certain to happen. A consequence analysis clearly shows that when left to their own decision-making, this group was destined to take off; their Timely, Positive and Certain consequences outweighed the Delayed, Negative and Uncertain consequences.

The "5 Whys" tool is a good way to help uncover the root cause of incidents. To do such an analysis, begin with the incident (what happened) and ask "why" five times to look for the root cause. If we were to do a "5 Whys" analysis of this incident with Tom, it might look like the following:

1. *Why did we crash and why did seven people die? Because we hit a mountain.*

2. *Why did we fly into the side of a mountain? Because we were off course, flying in fog.*

3. *Why were we flying in fog? Because we felt pressure to get to work and agreed to fly.*

4. *Why did we feel pressure? Because the fog was causing delays.*

5. *Why did we not wait longer? Because we perceived that the risk of a crash was low.*

The "5 Whys" root cause analysis is a useful tool, but it still does not get at the underpinning factors to explain WHY the pilot and passengers perceived that the risk of a crash was low. Starting with a "5 Whys" analysis and then doing a consequence analysis as we did above will lead to a more thorough root cause understanding.

In summary, after every behaviour we receive multiple consequences from different sources. To fully understand the consequences that encourage or discourage a behaviour, each one has to be analyzed for the source, the timeliness, whether it is wanted or unwanted, whether it is important or unimportant to the performer, and the level of certainty that it is going to occur. Notwithstanding the sources of the consequence, those that are Timely, Positive, Important and Certain will shape behaviours the fastest and most consistently.

It is these factors that lead us to the greatest hurdle in shaping a safety culture: the majority of unsafe acts do not result in injury, therefore the negative consequence associated with them are UNCERTAIN. Furthermore, the majority of unsafe acts have Timely, Positive, Important and Certain outcomes. For example, people who take risks by taking some kind of shortcut are motivated to do so because of these kinds of positive consequences. When asked about this, their typical response is, "I have done it this way many times and never got hurt." They are right; they may have done that task that way many times or even for many years. However, that does not mean that they have been safe, it only means that they have been lucky.

Classification of Incidents

For decades, many organizations have been using a tool known as Heinrich's Safety Pyramid to help assess their level of safety. There is a myth embedded in this practice. Heinrich's pyramid is not a predictive model – it is simply a rearward-looking form of Pareto analysis. Using the safety pyramid to assess the level of site safety may lead to inaccurate assumptions.

Many people may recall the day that the Deepwater Horizon drilling platform blew up in the Gulf of Mexico, killing nine workers and causing one of the world's largest marine oil disasters. That same day, the crew on board was celebrating their safety record. Using the safety pyramid approach (low number of lost time injuries and fatalities), the rig appeared to be a safe working environment. However, the investigation into the disaster found a number of procedural violations, a lack of managerial oversight for safety, and many other behavioural shortcomings which culminated in the incident. The rig was clearly not a safe working environment; they had simply been lucky to prevent injuries for a period previous to the explosion.

To examine the myth of the safety pyramid as a predictive model more closely, let's parse the types of safety incidents into two broad classifications at opposite ends of the spectrum.

At one end of the spectrum are high frequency/low severity incidents. These kind of frequent incidents might be considered "minor" in nature (a twisted ankle or a sliver in a finger) if, and only if, the particular incident has low potential to result in serious bodily harm or fatality. For example, a twisted ankle that results from tripping over a piece of wood on the floor is likely a low severity incident. A twisted ankle that results from leaping out of a moving truck moments before it crashes into a high-speed train would not be considered a low severity incident as the overall outcome could have resulted in fatality.

At the other end of the spectrum are low frequency/high severity incidents. While they do not occur very often, these kind of incidents have the potential to culminate in serious bodily harm or fatality. An aircraft crash is a good example of such an incident.

If all such incidents are analyzed together using a safety pyramid approach, the low frequency/high severity incidents are masked and can become overlooked amongst the volume of high frequency/low severity incidents.

To create a true safety culture, these different classifications of incidents must be addressed separately. While a behavioural approach is effective at correcting both classifications of incidents, the necessary antecedents and consequences are very different.

In Tom's case, the moment of impact when the pilot asked if anyone wanted to get off the plane because they were uncomfortable with low-level flying was indeed an infrequent situation, but one that unfortunately had very high severity. If the airline had been using a proper behaviour-based safety approach, the plane would never have been allowed to take off.

I would like to share one final thought regarding the central theme of this book: "moments of impact". Incident investigations are all rearward-looking, just like the data in a safety pyramid. The damage has already been done, and someone has already been injured when these things are used.

To create a global safety culture, we need focus on things that are forward-looking rather than rearward-looking.

Having meaningful safety conversations with one another, and creating moments of impact, are key to safety and the creation of a safe work culture. How do we know that we have indeed had a moment of impact? Quite simply, by observing what the performer chooses to do of their own volition.

Let me make another clear distinction here; I am not talking about simply telling others to be safe. If you clearly outline your expectations for how a task is to be done, and then stand there to observe a performer doing it, there is a high likelihood that the person will attempt to follow your instructions. You have simply paired an antecedent (your clear verbal expectation) with a timely consequence (observing them) to achieve temporary *compliance* with your request. This does not mean that you have achieved lasting behaviour change in the performer.

We know that for the most part, "telling" and "reminding" are both ineffective ways to achieve lasting behaviour change. "Reminding" times the frequency with which we remind, equates to nagging – a negative consequence that actually pushes the performer away from the very behaviour that we are trying to encourage. My good friend Josep Tura sums up this conundrum as follows: "Behaviour change is a door that is opened from the inside."

Impactful leaders do more asking than telling. They ask others good open-ended questions, and engage others in meaningful conversations to talk through potential risks. The real moment of impact occurs when a person comes to their own conclusion that there is a safer way to perform a task, and commits to it.

YOUR JOURNEY

I hope that reading my story has helped you, or will help you in the future, to think about your own safety, and the safety of those around you in a new way.

I wish you safe journeys throughout your entire life.

Whether that journey is to or from work. Whether that journey is simply the journey of daily tasks: mowing your lawn, going down stairs, picking up your children from school.

The next time that even the simplest task does not feel right somehow, what will you do?

Will you get off the plane?

I wish you many safe and positive moments of impact; sharing life lessons with co-workers, grandchildren, a neighbour, a stranger.

Go in peace. Go safely.

Tom

Tom speaking to a group of industrial workers in 2014.
Photograph by Bob Nyen

10420225R00083

Made in the USA
Monee, IL
28 August 2019

MOMENTS OF IMPACT

Moments of Impact is the true story of Tom Wilson, the sole survivor of a plane crash that killed seven others. Badly burned and alone on a mountainous uninhabited island in British Columbia on a cold November day, Tom had the fight of his life on his hands.

Join Tom on this journey as he shares his story of survival, spirituality, and the search for meaning in the face of disaster, and his newfound quest to make the world a safer place.

"If you are responsible for industrial safety you need to read this book. The safety culture you have created will influence the critical on-the-job decisions your employees make."

Brett Hollbrook - Vice President Central Appalachia Operations, CONSOL Energy

"A truly gut wrenching story that grabs your attention. Great perspectives on why people do the things they do and the insights on how to make the world a safer place. Our company has used these principles and have become leaders in our industry in the area of personal safety."

Mark Neas - President Brand Energy Solutions

A portion of all book proceeds will be donated to the University of Alberta Hospital Burn Ward.

University Hospital Foundation

Supporting
University of Alberta Hospital
Mazankowski Alberta Heart Institute
Kaye Edmonton Clinic

$29.95

Follow us on Facebook:
Moments of Impact
The International Safety Institute
www.insafein.com

ISBN 9781511768269

90000 >

9 781511 768269